Day Wal
SouthP

20 routes in West Yorkshire and beyond

Vertebrate Publishing, Sheffield
www.**v-publishing**.co.uk

Day Walks in the SouthPennines

20 routes in West
Yorkshire and beyond

Paul Besley

Day Walks in the SouthPennines

20 routes in West Yorkshire and beyond

 First published in 2020 by **Vertebrate Publishing.**

Vertebrate Publishing, Omega Court, 352 Cemetery Road,
Sheffield S11 8FT, United Kingdom.
www.v-publishing.co.uk

A CIP catalogue record for this book is available from the British Library.

ISBN 978-1-912560-65-3

Front cover: The Wessenden Valley in golden hour (route 6).
Back cover: Standedge Tunnels at Tunnel End, Marsden (route 4).
Photography by **Paul Besley** unless otherwise credited.

 All maps reproduced by permission of Ordnance Survey on behalf
of The Controller of Her Majesty's Stationery Office.
© Crown Copyright. 100025218

Design by Nathan Ryder, production by Cameron Bonser.
www.v-publishing.co.uk

Printed and bound in Europe by Pulsio.
Vertebrate Publishing is committed to printing on paper from sustainable sources.

Contents

AN OLD PACKHORSE TRACK ACROSS THE MOORS

Introduction

The South Pennines is a secret. A landscape hidden in full view, passed everyday by thousands of unsuspecting people. Cross the Pennines by the M62 and you slice through the area unknowing of the delicacies that lay within. This is a land of wilderness, rough moorland, deep valleys and big skies. It is not a barren land held in perpetuity to a past time; this is a landscape that is constantly evolving. Industry has played a big part. This is cotton and wool country. Once the source of textiles that draped the world and also the growing pains of the Industrial Revolution. The South Pennines is where society began; the Co-operative Group, the building societies, the trade unions and even the NHS can find roots here. Then came the sadness of the silent mill, sitting in the valley, unused, forgotten. There was a time not so long ago when this place was abandoned, no longer of use to the world.

But it is now resurgent with a new zest for life. The landscape breathes and lives with the communities that dot its surface like the crystals of quartz in gritstone. It is the people who have made this place interesting, have brought it back to life. As you walk the landscape you can feel that sense of togetherness, see a pride in place. A line of sparkling white washing hung out to dry on a blustery moor would be incongruous anywhere else. But not in the South Pennines.

You walk with this landscape taking with you whatever it has to give that day: a poem to rain, cotton grass on Black Hill or the autumnal golden hour in Hebden Dale, the trees on fire with golds and yellows and rich browns. And I think we also give a little of ourselves back by simply enjoying being there and savouring the memory of our encounter. Imagine a walk that takes in the landscape mixed with literature and art, and at the end a brass band outside a pub with real ale. That is the South Pennines.

Paul Besley

Acknowledgements

I would like to thank William Hall, Mel Bale, David Haffenden, Andy Leader and Tammany Batty for their invaluable suggestions, help and knowledge of the South Pennines. The Peak & Northern Footpath Society for help with footpaths and rights of way. The team at Vertebrate Publishing, Jon Barton, John Coefield, and particularly my editor, Helen Parry. Also, Alison Counsell who accompanied me on many of the walks and made helpful suggestions. Finally Scout, my walking companion on all the routes, who probably walked twice as far and complained half as much.

About the walks

The South Pennines area covered by this book is bounded by the M61 to the west, the A59 and the A65 to the north, a line between Holmfirth and Keighley in to the east and the A628 to the south. Most of the walking is over moorland and deep valleys. I have endeavoured to plan walks that set off from places of habitation where possible with good transport links, otherwise the start is but a short walk from a transport connection. As the area is relatively small the book has been divided in to southern and northern sections. My one piece of important advice is to check for access at **www.openaccess.naturalengland. org.uk** before setting off for a walk. Do not attempt a walk if shooting is taking place.

All the walks can be completed in one day and I have tried to group walks so that a weekend break can be planned with walks in the same area.

Walk times

Walk times are based on a walking speed of four kilometres per hour and using Naismith's rule for ascent. If a walk goes off path across moorland this can add time. No time has been allowed for breaks. In winter always allow extra time.

Navigation

The South Pennines is a large area and is covered in full by a number of Ordnance Survey (OS) Explorer 1:25,000 or OS Landranger 1:50,000 maps. The book has detailed maps and directions, however a map is always useful along with a compass. Some sections are over featureless terrain and it is helpful to be able to identify points off the guidebook map that can aid navigation.

The routes in this guidebook are covered by the following maps in the OS Explorer 1:25,000 series:

OL1 Peak District: Dark Peak Area
OL21 South Pennines
287 West Pennine Moors
297 Lower Wharfedale & Washburn Valley

GPS and mobile phones

A GPS device is always useful. If this is on a mobile phone carry a powerpack to prevent the battery from going flat. Smartphones are particularly useful if an emergency arises as it can aid rescuers in locating the phone's position if a signal is present. Much of the area has good phone signal coverage but there are always blind spots. If you need to make a call, try and get to high ground for a signal.

Footpaths and rights of way

Most of the walks are along public rights of way and should have no restriction. If there are these need to be reported to the relevant local authority who will investigate. Parts of some walks go across open access moorland with no path. I am a firm believer in getting away from the beaten path to explore areas generally not visited by other people. Much of the land is shooting land for grouse and at certain times of year will legally be closed to the public with the exception of public rights of way. Always check **www.openaccess. naturalengland.org.uk** for any closures before setting off.

Comfort

While out walking to research this guidebook I wore boots or trail shoes, and sometimes I needed gaiters; I always wore long trousers to prevent tick bites. It can get cold on the hills, especially with a strong wind, so I always carried extra clothing. My rucksack is always packed to allow me to spend the night in relative comfort should conditions dictate. I also carry a survival tent should I need to bivvy down in bad weather. Spare food and drink are a must. Some people find walking poles useful and they certainly help negotiate the 'Turk's heads' – large tufts of grass that cover the moors.

Safety

This is a landscape of high moorland and deep valleys. The weather can turn quickly changing a moderate day into a bad weather day. Always be prepared. Leave details of your route with a person who knows what to do if you have not returned by a certain time. Never leave things to chance. After heavy rain the streams and rivers can be swollen and the moors sodden, this may change a walk and allowances should be made to change the route – another good reason for carrying a map. In winter daylight hours are shorter so ensure you have a torch handy along with spare batteries. It is often easier to spot a light than hear a whistle, so a torch is also useful for attracting rescuers in an emergency. Remember. You CAN always turn back. Beware of ticks and carry a removal tool. Always seek medical advice if you think you have been bitten.

Rescue

Should the worst happen – and it can happen to the best – remain calm. Dial **999** and ask for **Police** and then **Mountain Rescue**. Try to have a six-figure grid reference of your location or that of your casualty. It may take time for rescuers to reach you, but they will come, so remain where you are and do not attempt to move. Keep a phone channel free for rescuers to contact you. If you don't have phone reception try to attract the attention of others nearby. The standard distress signal is six short blasts on a whistle every minute.

Emergency rescue by SMS text

In the UK you can also contact the emergency services by SMS text – useful if you have low battery or intermittent signal. You need to register your phone first by texting **'register'** to 999 and then following the instructions in the reply. **Do it now** – it could save yours or someone else's life. **www.emergencysms.net**

The Countryside Code

Respect other people

Please respect the local community and other people using the outdoors.
Remember your actions can affect people's lives and livelihoods.

Consider the local community and other people enjoying the outdoors

» Respect the needs of local people and visitors alike – for example, don't block gateways, driveways or other paths with your vehicle.

» When riding a bike or driving a vehicle, slow down or stop for horses, walkers and farm animals and give them plenty of room. By law, cyclists must give way to walkers and horse riders on bridleways.

» Co-operate with people at work in the countryside. For example, keep out of the way when farm animals are being gathered or moved and follow directions from the farmer.

» Busy traffic on small country roads can be unpleasant and dangerous to local people, visitors and wildlife – so slow down and, where possible, leave your vehicle at home, consider sharing lifts and use alternatives such as public transport or cycling. For public transport information, phone Traveline on 0871 200 22 33 or visit **www.traveline.info**

Leave gates and property as you find them and follow paths unless wider access is available

» A farmer will normally close gates to keep farm animals in, but may sometimes leave them open so the animals can reach food and water. Leave gates as you find them or follow instructions on signs. When in a group, make sure the last person knows how to leave the gates.

» Follow paths unless wider access is available, such as on open country or registered common land (known as 'open access' land).

» If you think a sign is illegal or misleading, such as a *Private – No Entry* sign on a public path, contact the local authority.

» Leave machinery and farm animals alone – don't interfere with animals even if you think they're in distress. Try to alert the farmer instead.

» Use gates, stiles or gaps in field boundaries if you can – climbing over walls, hedges and fences can damage them and increase the risk of farm animals escaping.

» Our heritage matters to all of us – be careful not to disturb ruins and historic sites.

Protect the natural environment

We all have a responsibility to protect the countryside now and for future generations, so make sure you don't harm animals, birds, plants or trees and try to leave no trace of your visit. When out with your dog make sure it is not a danger or nuisance to farm animals, horses, wildlife or other people.

Leave no trace of your visit and take your litter home

» Protecting the natural environment means taking special care not to damage, destroy or remove features such as rocks, plants and trees. They provide homes and food for wildlife, and add to everybody's enjoyment of the countryside.

» Litter and leftover food doesn't just spoil the beauty of the countryside, it can be dangerous to wildlife and farm animals – so take your litter home with you. Dropping litter and dumping rubbish are criminal offences.

» Fires can be as devastating to wildlife and habitats as they are to people and property – so be careful with naked flames and cigarettes at any time of the year. Sometimes, controlled fires are used to manage vegetation, particularly on heaths and moors between 1 October and 15 April, but if a fire appears to be unattended then report it by calling **999**.

Keep dogs under effective control

When you take your dog into the outdoors, always ensure it does not disturb wildlife, farm animals, horses or other people by keeping it under effective control. This means that you:

» keep your dog on a lead, or

» keep it in sight at all times, be aware of what it's doing and be confident it will return to you promptly on command

» ensure it does not stray off the path or area where you have a right of access

Special dog rules may apply in particular situations, so always look out for local signs – for example:

» dogs may be banned from certain areas that people use, or there may be restrictions, byelaws or control orders limiting where they can go

» the access rights that normally apply to open country and registered common land (known as 'open access' land) require dogs to be kept on a short lead between 1 March and 31 July, to help protect ground-nesting birds, and all year round near farm animals

» at the coast, there may also be some local restrictions to require dogs to be kept on a short lead during the bird breeding season, and to prevent disturbance to flocks of resting and feeding birds during other times of year

It's always good practice (and a legal requirement on 'open access' land) to keep your dog on a lead around farm animals and horses, for your own safety and for the welfare of the animals. A farmer may shoot a dog which is attacking or chasing farm animals without being liable to compensate the dog's owner.

However, if cattle or horses chase you and your dog, it is safer to let your dog off the lead – don't risk getting hurt by trying to protect it. Your dog will be much safer if you let it run away from a farm animal in these circumstances and so will you.

Everyone knows how unpleasant dog mess is and it can cause infections, so always clean up after your dog and get rid of the mess responsibly – 'bag it and bin it'. Make sure your dog is wormed regularly to protect it, other animals and people.

Enjoy the outdoors
Even when going out locally, it's best to get the latest information about where and when you can go. For example, your rights to go on to some areas of open access land and coastal land may be restricted in particular places at particular times. Find out as much as you can about where you are going, plan ahead and follow advice and local signs.

Plan ahead and be prepared
You'll get more from your visit if you refer to up-to-date maps or guidebooks and websites before you go. Visit **www.gov.uk/natural-england** or contact local information centres or libraries for a list of outdoor recreation groups offering advice on specialist activities.

You're responsible for your own safety and for others in your care – especially children – so be prepared for natural hazards, changes in weather and other events. Wild animals, farm animals and horses can behave unpredictably if you get too close, especially if they're with their young – so give them plenty of space.

Check weather forecasts before you leave. Conditions can change rapidly especially on mountains and along the coast, so don't be afraid to turn back. When visiting the coast check for tide times on **www.ukho.gov.uk/easytide** – don't risk getting cut off by rising tides and take care on slippery rocks and seaweed.

Part of the appeal of the countryside is that you can get away from it all. You may not see anyone for hours, and there are many places without clear mobile phone signals, so let someone else know where you're going and when you expect to return.

Follow advice and local signs

England has about 190,000km (118,000 miles) of public rights of way, providing many opportunities to enjoy the natural environment. Get to know the signs and symbols used in the countryside to show paths and open countryside.

How to use this book

This book should provide you with all of the information that you need for an enjoyable, trouble-free and successful walk. The following tips should also be of help:

» We strongly recommend that you invest in the relevant maps listed on page ix. These are essential even if you are familiar with the area – you may need to cut short the walk or take an alternative route.

» Choose your route. Consider the time you have available and the abilities/level of experience of all members of your party – then read the Safety section of this guide.

» We recommend that you study the route description carefully before setting off. Cross-reference this with your map so that you've got a good sense of general orientation in case you need an escape route. Make sure that you are familiar with the symbols used on the maps.

» Get out there and get walking!

Maps, descriptions, distances

While every effort has been made to maintain accuracy within the maps and descriptions in this guidebook, we have had to process a vast amount of information and we are unable to guarantee that every single detail is correct. Please exercise caution if a direction appears at odds with the route on the map. If in doubt, a comparison between the route, the description and a quick cross-reference with your map (along with a bit of common sense) should help ensure that you're on the right track. Note that distances have been measured off the map, and map distances rarely coincide 100 per cent with distances on the ground. Please treat stated distances as a guideline only.

Ordnance Survey maps are the most commonly used, are easy to read and many people are happy using them. If you're not familiar with OS maps and are unsure of what the symbols mean, you can download a free OS 1:25,000 map legend from **www.ordnancesurvey.co.uk**

Here are a few of the symbols and abbreviations we use on the maps and in our directions:

 ROUTE STARTING POINT   **ROUTE MARKER**   **SHORTCUT**

 OPTIONAL ROUTE   52 **ADDITIONAL GRID LINE NUMBERS TO AID NAVIGATION**

Km/mile conversion chart

Metric to Imperial

1 kilometre [km]	1,000 m	0.6214 mile
1 metre [m]	100 cm	1.0936 yd
1 centimetre [cm]	10 mm	0.3937 in
1 millimetre [mm]		0.03937 in

Imperial to Metric

1 mile	1,760 yd	1.6093 km
1 yard [yd]	3 ft	0.9144 m
1 foot [ft]	12 in	0.3048 m
1 inch [in]		2.54 cm

Day Walks in the
SouthPennines
Area Map & Route Finder

SECTION 1

The Southern Walks

The walks in this section cover the area from Holmfirth to Hebden Bridge. This is an area of high moorland and sparsely populated hill communities. It stretches across the county boundaries of Yorkshire and Lancashire and is dominated by the old cotton and wool mill towns of the South Pennines.

The views are spectacular, stretching down into the Snowdonia mountains and the landscape is often rugged and inspiring, demanding respect.

The communities are now resurgent after decades of decline and this has brought a vibrancy to the area that is refreshing.

The outlier of walk 10 (Rivington Pike and Winter Hill) in the Western Pennines has been included because, while being a short walk, the views to the south and west are amazing, in part due to the light that seems to be different from anywhere else.

THE SURPRISING RAMSDEN CLOUGH

COTTON GRASS ON BLACK HILL

01 **Holme to Black Hill**

14.1km/8.8miles

Solitude gradually envelops you during the ascent on to the high moors of Black Hill. The return journey across open moorland deposits you into the surprising glories of Ramsden Clough.

Brownhill Reservoir » Holme » Issues Road » Black Hill » Wrigley's Cabin » Holme Moss » Ramsden Clough » Brownhill Reservoir

Start
Car park by Ramsden Reservoir.
GR: SE 115056.

The Walk
The walk starts in the valley bottom and crosses the dam of Ramsden Reservoir before beginning the ascent to Black Hill. The first and only community we encounter is the Anglo-Saxon village of Holme. In the nineteenth century this became a thriving centre of weaving; many weavers' cottages can still be seen.

From Holme we enter the strange Issues Road, a long straight track that seemingly goes nowhere and is for no purpose. One of many such roads in the South Pennines that gave access to the common lands after being enclosed by private landowners. From there the route ascends to Black Hill, the third highest hill in the Peak District National Park. The triangulation pillar is known as Soldier's Lump, after the army engineers who erected the Ordnance Survey surveying station. A few years ago, it was surrounded by a thick black quagmire

of peat, caused by pollution from the mills of Manchester, but now the land is covered in wonderful cotton grass and other thick grasses.

Navigation will need to be good for the next section as there are no marked paths. From the triangulation pillar the walk heads over to the abandoned Wrigley's Cabin and then on to the Holme Moss Transmitting Station – always a good navigation point.

Finally, crossing the *Cote de Holme Moss*, of Tour de Yorkshire fame, after a short moorland crossing we enter Ramsden Clough. Ramsden Clough is somewhat of a shock to the eyes. This deep cleft in the moor gives spectacular views as the path works its way down to the valley bottom. Along the cliffs that line this section can often be found any number of raptors readying to quarter the skyline. Finally, the route descends to the car park via an ancient way that gives fine views down the Holme Valley to Holmfirth.

HOLME TO BLACK HILL

DISTANCE: 14.1KM/8.8MILES » **TOTAL ASCENT:** 450M/1,476FT » **START GR:** SE 115056 » **TIME:** ALLOW 5 HOURS **SATNAV:** HD9 2QE » **MAP:** OS EXPLORER OL1, PEAK DISTRICT: DARK PEAK AREA, 1:25,000 » **REFRESHMENTS:** THE FLEECE, HOLME » **NAVIGATION:** GOOD NAVIGATION SKILLS REQUIRED FOR MOORLAND SECTIONS.

SCOUT ON SOLDIER'S LUMP
TRIANGULATION PILLAR, BLACK HILL

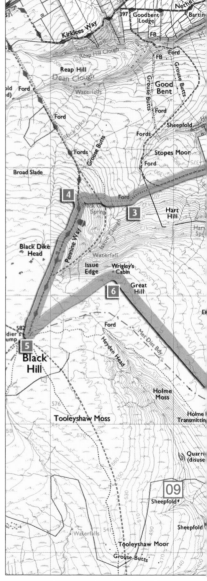

01 HOLME TO BLACK HILL

Directions – Holme to Black Hill

➔ **Turn right** out of the car park and walk down the road then **turn left** on the footpath across the dam of Ramsden Reservoir. At the end of the dam **bear right** to follow the footpath along the western side of Brownhill Reservoir, eventually crossing the footbridge by the waterfall in Rake Dike. Continue along the footpath as it curves to the right to gradually ascend the woodland to a stile. Cross the stile into a field and walk **diagonally left** uphill to a corner of the woodland. Go over a stone stile then along the footpath bounded by a wall to the left and a hedge to the right. At the end of the footpath go **left** through a gate then **turn right** following the wall line through a gate to eventually emerge on to the A6024 at Holme.

2 **Turn left** and pass Holme Castle to enter the village. Just before reaching the crest of the hill **turn right** over the cobbled area and join Meal Hill Road. Follow this road uphill past the school, continuing on as it becomes an unmade track. **Fork left** by Meal Hill on to Issues Road, a walled track heading south-west. Continue along the track, going through three gates, until you reach the stream descending from Issue Clough.

3 **Cross the stream** at the ford and **walk west** along the concessionary path up the hillside to reach the stone slabs of the Pennine Way by Black Grough Spring.

4 **Turn left** along the Pennine Way to arrive at the Ordnance Survey triangulation pillar at Soldier's Lump on the summit of Black Hill.

5 Take a **bearing of 52 degrees** and walk in that direction for **900m** to reach the remains of Wrigley's Cabin.

6 From the ruins take a **bearing of 138 degrees** and walk in that direction for **1.5km** to reach the Holme Moss Transmitting Station mast. **Turn left** and walk around the perimeter fence until you reach the A6024.

7 **Cross the road** to the car park; walk through the car park and to **go over a stile** and follow the footpath leading on to Fern Hill. Go over a stile and follow the fence line generally **east** for 2.3km to Ramsden Clough. **Cross the ford** and follow the footpath along the edge heading **north-east** until you reach the grouse shooting butts at Ruddle Clough.

8 **Cross the footbridge** and take the footpath heading **west** down Ruddle Clough then curving **north** along Ramsden Clough heading towards woodland. Keep to the concessionary path along the top of the woodland following it through the disused quarry and eventually enter a walled lane. Go through the gate and proceed along the lane until you come to the junction with the green lane known as Ramsden Road.

9 Continue straight on descending on the rough track. Just after the track curves to the left by Tinker Well **turn right** on to a footpath. Shortly afterwards **turn left** on to a fenced grassy lane which drops down the wooded hillside back to the car park by Ramsden Reservoir.

ENCLOSURE FIELDS ALONG ISSUES ROAD

REACHING THE TOP OF WILDERNESS GULLY WEST

Dove Stone Reservoir and Ashway Gap   11.2km/7miles

This rugged South Pennine landscape gives a sense of the original meaning of sublime; fearsome, awesome and utterly exhilarating. The ascent of Wilderness Gully West is a classic Peak scramble.

Dove Stone Reservoir » Chew Valley » Wilderness Gully West » Chew Reservoir » Cairn on Fox Stone » Ashway Gap » Dove Stone Reservoir

Start
Binn Green car park. GR: SE 018044.

The Walk
Beginning the walk around Dove Stone Reservoir gives the opportunity for a spot of bird watching in the surrounding RSPB nature reserve. This is a busy area full of people enjoying the stunning scenery and wildlife. As the route begins its ascent from the valley floor, climbing up the Chew Road towards the sky, a sense of foreboding combined with awe at the towering landscape envelops you.

The grade 1 scramble of Wilderness Gully West is a wonderful introduction to this strange pastime that bridges the gap between walking and climbing. The views from the top are stunning and a worthy prize for all that hard work. Skirting the top

of the Chew Valley brings you to Chew Reservoir, once the highest in England, then on to Dish Stone Moss before turning west across open moorland and a moderate test of navigation and compass skills to reach the edge path at Dish Stone Brow.

The names of some of the areas around the valley have macabre connotations, Charnel Clough and Dead Man's Lay-by are both connected with death. Moving along the edge path brings us to the Cairn on Fox Stone and a memorial to two climbers who fell in the Dolomites. Turning back into the moor brings you to the ford at Ashway Gap and the beginning of the descent to the valley floor and a return to Binn Green. This is a walk in the sublime tradition of our Victorian ancestors invoking fear and awe of this incredible landscape.

DOVE STONE RESERVOIR AND ASHWAY GAP

DISTANCE: 11.2KM/7MILES » **TOTAL ASCENT:** 442M/1,450FT » **START GR:** SE 018044 » **TIME:** ALLOW 4 HOURS **SATNAV:** OL3 7NN » **MAP:** OS EXPLORER OL1, PEAK DISTRICT: DARK PEAK AREA, 1:25,000 » **REFRESHMENTS:** THE CLARENCE, GREENFIELD » **NAVIGATION:** GOOD NAVIGATION SKILLS REQUIRED FOR MOORLAND SECTIONS.

Directions – Dove Stone Reservoir and Ashway Gap

➲ From the Binn Green car park take the footpath running **south** down through woodland to a stone stile. Cross the stile and **turn left** down a walled lane. Go through a gate and shortly afterwards **turn right** across Yeoman Hey Reservoir dam. Continue straight ahead to follow the wide track around the eastern side of Dove Stone Reservoir until you reach the junction with the southern reservoir track, just after crossing a bridge over a small stream.

2 **Bear left** and walk up Chew Road for 1.7km passing over a stile by a gate across the road along the way.

3 Begin to look for a comfortable **descent to Chew Brook** on the right; aim for the **right** of Wilderness Gully West which is the gully that is closest to Dove Stone Reservoir. Cross Chew Brook by the small footbridge between Chew Hurdles. Once across work your way to the base of Wilderness Gully West. This is a Grade 1 scramble so should be well within the competence of most walkers but, if in any doubt, use the optional route below. For those enjoying the scramble **work your way carefully to the top of the gully**, choosing the best line for your ability and the conditions of the day. The rock can be slippery when wet and alternative routes via the gully sides can be obtained. At the top of the gully **turn left** and head to Chew Reservoir.

▷OR To avoid the scramble continue **straight ahead** on Chew Road. The path curves round to the right to arrive at Chew Reservoir.

4 **Turn left** to head northwards across the dam to reach the Peak & Northern Footpath Society signpost.

5 **Turn left** to walk westwards to reach the edge path above Dish Stone Rocks.

6 The path curves round to the right; continue on **following the path** heading northwards to reach the Cairn on Fox Stone and the Great Dove Stone Rocks overlooking Dove Stone Reservoir. After passing the cairn continue along the edge path as it swings eastwards and you arrive at a stream.

7 **Cross the stream** below the waterfall at Ashway Gap and **continue walking northwards** until the path splits below the Ashway Stone.

8 Take the **left fork** to descend the hillside, **keeping to the right of the conduit** that feeds water into the reservoir. Go over the stile and walk down the steep slope to rejoin the eastern reservoir track.

9 **Turn right** and retrace your steps back to Binn Green car park.

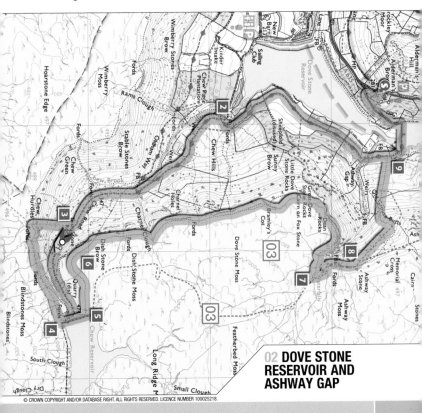

02 DOVE STONE RESERVOIR AND ASHWAY GAP

THE ORDNANCE SURVEY TRIANGULATION PILLAR ON BROADSTONE HILL

A walk across the northern tip of the Peak District National Park surrounded by the industrial revolution, the effects of world conflict and the Pennine Way – Britain's first National Trail.

Marsden » Standedge Trail » Pots and Pans » Broadstone Hill » Featherbed Moss » Black Moss » Pennine Way » Wessenden Valley » Marsden

Start
Marsden Station. GR: SE 047118.

The Walk

Marsden once resounded to the sound of the factory siren calling the workers to Bank Bottom Mill – if you were not inside the mill by 6.30 a.m. you did not work or receive pay. Today that industrial cathedral is silent, the weaving looms have gone and so have the workers. Marsden, like many mill towns in the South Pennines, has had to find a new purpose; the high moorland has provided a new focus for the arts to thrive in the community.

This walk initially follows the course of the Standedge Tunnels, a marvel of canal engineering that runs from Standedge to Diggle. Then the route heads south to the oddly named Pots and Pans and the striking war memorial that stands above the villages who lost men in both world wars.

Next the old Pennine Way is reached via the Cotton Famine Road across Featherbed Moss. This pointless road was built to provide work for starving cotton mill workers and their families during the American Civil War. It is a sombre moment walking along this moorland track that goes from nowhere to nowhere. However, the mood brightens as flagstones are reached and followed along the old National Trail to Black Moss Reservoir. Here the current Pennine Way route is joined and followed eastwards into the Wessenden Valley. The magnificent engineering achievement of the Butterley Reservoir and its famous spillway strike an imposing feature in this beautiful valley. From there the return to Marsden is through Bank Bottom Mill, where aficionados of industrial heritage can gaze upon a time now long past and imagine the throng of mill workers pouring down that narrow road; the mill looming above, the siren calling and the manager waiting to close the entrance to the stragglers pleading to be let in.

MARSDEN TO POTS AND PANS

DISTANCE: 22.3KM/13.9MILES » **TOTAL ASCENT:** 602M/1,975FT » **START GR:** SE 047118 » **TIME:** ALLOW 7 HOURS **SATNAV:** HD7 6AX » **MAP:** OS EXPLORER OL1, PEAK DISTRICT: DARK PEAK AREA, AND OL21, SOUTH PENNINES, 1:25,000 **REFRESHMENTS:** THE RIVERHEAD BREWERY TAP, MARSDEN » **NAVIGATION:** GOOD NAVIGATION SKILLS REQUIRED.

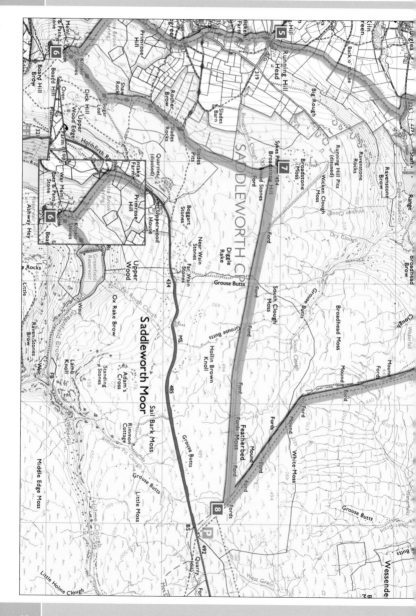

03 MARSDEN TO POTS AND PANS

Directions – Marsden to Pots and Pans

❻ From Marsden Station walk **south** down Station Road then **bear right** to join Church Lane. Walk past the church then **fork right** on to Town Gate. **Cross the A62** and go straight ahead on to Old Mount Road.

2 **Turn right** on to the first public footpath, walking uphill into trees. As the path sweeps **right** take the footpath on the **left** over the stile and follow the Peak & Northern Footpath Society sign along a sunken track to the right of a farm. Walk by a wall on your right-hand side through the farmyard to a gate. Follow the signs for *Standedge* along a grassy track until you reach the Standedge Trail. **Turn left** along the trail and walk for 1km until you reach Mount Road.

3 **Cross the road diagonally right** then follow the footpath sign on the **left** down the bank. Walk across the footbridge then go **right** up the steep bank and follow the wide grassy track generally **west** for 2km to pass through a gate leading on to a roadside car park. Continue straight ahead to walk along the path between the Brun Clough Reservoir and the A62.

4 Pass through a gate then **turn left** and follow the Standedge Trail **south** to a signpost then **south-west** along the Pennine Bridleway. Where the track splits by a tunnel airshaft **turn left** along the waymarked track to emerge in Diggle Edge. **Turn left** along the road and as it sweeps right follow the drive on the **left** between buildings then exit into fields. Continue **south-east** until you reach a tarmac lane leading to Diggle. Go **straight ahead** to the next junction then **turn left**. Just after crossing a bridge **turn right** over the stile on to a footpath. Follow the path initially **south-west**, along the fence line on your left-hand side to a stone stile, continuing on **south** now following a stone wall on your right-hand side then **south-west** to a walled lane. **Turn right** then **turn left** on to a footpath heading **south-west** across several fields to the minor road at Running Hill Head.

5 Cross the road and take the footpath **south** to Pobgreen. On reaching a tarmac lane **turn left** up to the junction then go **diagonally right** and over a wooden stile on the opposite side of the road. Follow the footpath **south-east** to the right-hand side of a house. Go through the gate and continue straight ahead in front of weavers' cottages. **Bear right** walking across the front of a row of houses and follow the footpath **south-west** to a wall corner with a stream running down to a house. **Turn left** here and follow the footpath up through the disused quarry to reach the war memorial at Pots and Pans.

6 From the memorial take the footpath **north-east** then cross a stile and follow the track uphill to arrive at a small white post marking the position of a pipeline on Sugar Loaf. **Turn left** and follow the footpath **north-east** to arrive at the Ordnance Survey triangulation pillar on Broadstone Hill.

7 Walk directly **east** from the triangulation pillar to the raised embankment of the Cotton Famine Road. Follow the structure **east** until you meet the stone flags of the old Pennine Way at Featherbed Moss.

8 **Turn left** and proceed along the footpath to Black Moss Reservoir.

9 **Turn right** to walk along the **south-east** edge of the reservoir. **Turn right** along the stone flags following the Pennine Way **east** down Blakely Clough to reach the Wessenden Valley.

10 Drop down the steep hillside path keeping to the Pennine Way and cross Wessenden Brook, ascending the eastern bank to the wide track. **Turn left** along the track; the track becomes a road and you pass the Butterley Reservoir spillway. Continue along the road then **descend steps on the left** to the bottom of the spillway. Walk along the tarmac road leaving the reservoir and continue on as it passes between the abandoned buildings of Bank Bottom Mill to arrive at a junction with a road.

11 **Turn left** and follow the road straight ahead over the roundabout then **bear left** to pass under a bridge. Continue **straight ahead** into Church Lane then **turn left** along Station Road to return to Marsden Station.

04 **Marsden to Northern Rotcher** 14.7km/9.1miles

Heritage and art are all to be found on a walk that affirms the connection between the landscape and the humans that live, work, and play within it.

Marsden » Tunnel End » March Haigh Reservoir » Northern Rotcher » Standedge » Pule Hill » Firth Pule » Marsden

Start

Marsden Station. GR: SE 047118.

The Walk

Perhaps of all the walks in the book this one speaks of the South Pennines the most. The area is not a national park and at first glance this may seem a negative aspect. But this walk demonstrates how a living landscape that is constantly developing is a beautiful place.

The walk starts via the canal towpath to Tunnel End, an odd name for a place but one that is very descriptive as it is indeed the end of the Standedge Tunnels. Heading west through tiny hillside hamlets full of weavers' cottages with their rows of tiny windows, the route opens out on to the moors above Marsden. This is good walking along easy footpaths and trails to the edge of Northern Rotcher, the name indicating the local influence of the Normans almost a thousand years ago. The views from here are magnificent, stretching as they do into the Peak District and Snowdonia national parks. In the valley below is the remains of the Roman fort at Castleshaw.

Moving on, the Pennine Way guides us by the Ordnance Survey triangulation pillar and the Dinner Stone – one of the strange rock formations from the gritstone cap that tops these hills. From there a descent along the old packhorse road that ran between Yorkshire and Lancashire goes across the eighteenth-century Thieves Clough Bridge and the only steep ascent of the day on to Pule Hill. Descending from this high point into the quarry below, the work of poet laureate Simon Armitage can be found, his words carved into the black encrusted Pennine gritstone. Leaving this place of contemplation, the route heads for home, stopping at a military memorial that stands guard above Marsden to admire the living landscape that is the South Pennines.

MARSDEN TO NORTHERN ROTCHER

DISTANCE: 14.7KM/9.1MILES » **TOTAL ASCENT:** 424M/1,391FT » **START GR:** SE 047118 » **TIME:** ALLOW 5 HOURS **SATNAV:** HD7 6AX » **MAP:** OS EXPLORER OL1, PEAK DISTRICT: DARK PEAK AREA, 1:25,000 » **REFRESHMENTS:** WATERSEDGE CAFE, MARSDEN » **NAVIGATION:** AVERAGE NAVIGATION SKILLS REQUIRED.

Directions – Marsden to Northern Rotcher

➤ From Marsden Station take the canal towpath **west** to Tunnel End. **Cross the canal bridge** then go through the car park and walk up the grassy slope on the **left**. When you reach a lane **turn right** and walk along it until you reach a junction with Waters Road. Go **straight on**, heading **north-east**, to take the public footpath that rises up steps through a private garden on the left of a house. Exit via a wrought iron gate on to an unmade road.

2 **Turn left** along the lane; pass through Berry Greave **bearing left** at the fork then **bear right** at the next fork. As the lane turns sharp right and passes a farm building on the left continue along the walled grassy track through a gate to open land. Follow the gently rising footpath **north-west** around Great Edge, then where the path becomes paved follow it **south-west** over a stream and up a short slope to a minor road.

3 **Turn right** following the road through Lower Green Owlers until the tarmac ends, then **turn left** along a track until the track splits. Take the **left-hand** track uphill to a stile by a farm gate on the left. **Cross the stile** and follow the footpath **north-west** towards March Haigh Reservoir. Go over the bridge at the foot of the dam and ascend the steep bank to meet the bridleway coming up Willykay Clough.

4 **Turn right** along the bridleway and walk for 1.3km to reach a path junction. **Turn left** and walk for a short distance then **turn left** along the Pennine Way to ascend the hill and arrive at Northern Rotcher.

5 Follow the path along the gritstone edge **south-east** passing the Dinner Stone and triangulation pillar and leave Millstone Edge via a gate. Cross a walled field, walking over the remains of a wall to arrive at a second gate with a tall signpost beyond. **Turn left** and follow the footpath over a stile on to the National Trust Marsden Moor Estate. Follow a paved path down Thieves Clough, crossing Thieves Clough Bridge then **bearing right** to ford the stream. Continue on and go through a gate to arrive at the A62 by the Great Western Inn.

6 **Cross the road** then continue straight ahead to go **over the stile** then walk along the dam of Redbrook Reservoir to a small footbridge at the end. **Cross the footbridge** then walk **east** across the moor along a path following the line of a drain maintaining course. The path swings to the north-east to arrive at a road. **Turn left** along the road then **turn right** on a footpath signposted to the *Standedge Trail* and *Pule Hill*. By the duckboards **turn right** to leave the Standedge Trail and ascend the footpath to the top of Pule Hill.

7 From the Marsden Estate marker stone on top of Pule Hill, descend at a convenient place to the base of the crag and walk **north** along uneven ground past a series of interesting caves and rock formations to arrive at the Snow Stone, part of the Stanza Stones poetry trail.

    ▶OR▶ Continue **north** along the gritstone edge until you reach the steep incline rising from the road. Then, descending the sloping path to the top of the remains of the incline winding house, continue **south** into the quarry and keeping to the western side arrive at the Snow Stone and the Poetry Seat, part of the Stanza Stones poetry trail.

8 After visiting the poetry of Simon Armitage **ascend the incline** and **turn left** at the top to follow the footpath around Firth Pule and past an air shaft for the Standedge Tunnels to reach a small cross commemorating the Duke of Wellington's Regiment at the top of a hill. Descend the hill **north-east**, making the best of it through boggy ground, and exit via a gate on to a stone track.

9 **Turn right** on the stone track through Intake Head Farm and head **south-east** across duckboards to descend over a low wall into a small clough. Cross the stream and enter a wooded area via a gate, then rise up steps taking the path to a stile. **Cross the stile** into a walled and fenced corridor; **cross a second stile** then reach a gate on the left. **Go through the gate** and descend the hillside keeping within the walled lane until you reach a stile on the right. **Cross the stile** and follow the wall **south-east** to a stream. **Do not cross the stream** but go to the right of the wall then **go through the gate** on the left at the wall junction. Follow the line of the wall to a farm.

10 **Turn left** and follow the footpath through the farm walking down the hillside at the side of a stream to reach a wooden stile. **Cross the stile** and walk through trees to a lane. **Turn right** along the lane and **turn left** at a road junction. Cross the A62 and walk straight ahead along the road passing the church on the left. **Turn left** along Station Road to reach Marsden Station.

SCOUT CAVING ON PULE HILL

05 **Denshaw to White Hill**   16.3km/10.1miles

Denshaw is one of the Saddleworth towns that hold a brass band contest on Whit Friday
– the perfect time to do this walk.

Denshaw » Castleshaw Moor » White Hill » Windy Hill » Ogden Reservoir » Lower Ogden »
Edge Gate » Denshaw

Start

The Junction Inn, Denshaw. GR: SD 974106.

The Walk

Denshaw is one of the villages that form
the Saddleworth group of communities
which lie at the foot of the high South
Pennine moors. A great day to undertake
this walk is Whit Friday, when villages
around Saddleworth hold brass band
contests, with dozens of bands from across
the world taking part. It makes for a won-
derfully unique carnival atmosphere.

Set off early from The Junction Inn, the
former posting house in the centre of
Denshaw. Very quickly you are away from
civilisation and ascending Moor Lane across
Castleshaw Moor to the Pennine Way at
Northern Rotcher. Heading north to cross
the A640 the Pennine Way then heads
north-west and the walk reaches its highest
point at the triangulation pillar at White Hill.

Continuing along the Pennine Way you
become aware of a rumbling sound as the
M62 comes into view, along with the
communication mast on Rook Stones Hill.
Here the route leaves the Pennine Way and
heads west with excellent views across
Lancashire and amazingly the sound of the
M62 becoming lost in the expansive
landscape. The old bridleway works its way
west across several hilltops before joining
the concessionary path down to Ogden
Reservoir. This is gentle walking with
wonderful views to both sides of the
Pennines.

The final leg back to Denshaw goes through
Higher Ogden, a typical hillside community,
before descending across the pastures back
to The Junction Inn and the brass band
contest.

DENSHAW TO WHITE HILL

DISTANCE: 16.3KM/10.1MILES » **TOTAL ASCENT:** 449M/1,473FT » **START GR:** SD 974106 » **TIME:** ALLOW 5 HOURS
SATNAV: OL3 5SE » **MAP:** OS EXPLORER OL21, SOUTH PENNINES, 1:25,000 » **REFRESHMENTS:** THE JUNCTION INN,
DENSHAW » **NAVIGATION:** GOOD NAVIGATION SKILLS REQUIRED.

05 DENSHAW TO WHITE HILL

Directions – Denshaw to White Hill

➔ From The Junction Inn on the junction of the A672 and A640 go **south-east** along the A640 and **turn left** along the lane immediately before the Oddfellows Club. Follow the lane past the club car park until it splits higher up. Take the **right-hand fork** towards the rear corner of the farm buildings. **Turn left** up a short walled track then bear **south-east** across fields initially following a wall then dropping down through open fields to a gate giving access on to the A640 Huddersfield Road.

2 Cross the road and go through a gate and walk across the dam of New Years Bridge Reservoir. At the far end of the dam **bear left**, keeping to the **north-west** side of the stone wall. At the stile in the wall **turn right** and follow the fingerposts **south-east** uphill until you reach a wooden stile giving access to the Moor Lane track.

3 Go **left** through the gate and follow the walled track **north-east** to a wooden gate leading on to open moorland. Maintain a **north-easterly** then **northerly** direction as you ascend the hillside for 650m then turn **east** across Hind Hill following the Oldham Way eventually **south-east** to its junction with the Pennine Way.

4 **Turn left** along the Pennine Way and exit the moor via a wooden gate on to the A640. **Cross the road bearing left** and **turn right** following the fingerposts on to Marsden Moor. Continue along the Pennine Way crossing a stile by the old Lancashire boundary stone until you reach the Ordnance Survey triangulation pillar on White Hill.

5 Keep to the **left** of the sheep fence as you walk **north-west** along the trail passing through gates as the trail heads **north** to bring you to the A672. Cross the road and walk towards the communications mast, passing between it and the A672 to go through a wooden gate.

6 **Turn left** after the gate and follow the track **south-west** downhill to gain a track with the right-hand wall still standing but the left-hand wall only just visible among the grass. Continue along the track for 2km finally passing through a metal gate to arrive at a track junction.

7   **Turn right** and follow the fingerpost pointing the way to *Hollingworth Lake* along the Rochdale Way. On reaching the junction of Tunshill Lane and the concessionary path to Ogden Reservoir **bear left** and follow the track **south** to the reservoir. Cross the dam then **turn left** along the road to reach a car park.

8   Cross the road and take the footpath **south-east** to Lower Ogden. At the hamlet **turn left** uphill then **turn right** along a cobbled road that runs between houses to reach a farm track. **Turn left** along the track as it rises gently to a junction with a tarmac lane. **Turn left** along the lane **bearing right** at Edge Gate Farm to descend to the A640.

9   **Cross the road; turn left** to walk along the road then immediately **turn right** on to the footpath between houses to a wooden gate. Go through the gate and immediately **turn left** following the fingerpost **south-east** across fields, passing across the driveway of Cherry Clough Nursery. Continue **south-east** aiming to the **right** of a house. Go through a gate following the waymarkers to a narrow tarmac drive. **Turn left** along the road until just before a set of electric gates. Take the footpath on the **left** down a steep banking and exit on to the A672. **Turn left** along the road to return to The Junction Inn.

THE VIEW ACROSS THE ROMAN CAMP AT CASTLESHAW

THE WESSENDEN VALLEY IN GOLDEN HOUR

06 **Meltham to West Nab**

15km/9.3miles

A walk that shows off the amazing views of the South Pennine landscape: wide vistas from gritstone outcrops and far off horizons down the long valleys.

Meltham » Royd Edge » West Nab » Leyzing Clough » Wessenden Valley » Black Edge » Shooters Nab » Meltham

Start

St Bartholomew's Church, Meltham.
GR: SE 099106.

The Walk

Meltham is a bustling little Pennine town that was once an industrial powerhouse, being the home to a huge silk mill which employed over 1,000 people in its heyday and also to David Brown Tractors. David Brown went on to own Aston Martin cars and gave his initials DB to the now famous mark.

This walk soon leaves the town behind and quickly heads out on to the moors along a pleasant track that takes the walker along Royd Edge with excellent views of typical South Pennine hill farms. Once across Wessenden Head Road and past the Cock Crowing Stone, which is said to crow when the stones on top of the hill move during the solstice, there is a short ascent to West Nab and Raven Rocks. There are several rock features around the summit which bear examination for the shapes made by weathering on this exposed hill. The views

across the South Pennines from the triangulation pillar are expansive and give a sense of the size of the whole area.

Dropping down into the Wessenden Valley the walk follows the reservoirs downstream, keeping to the high footpath to maintain the views. Eventually the trail delivers you above Marsden and the giant Bank Bottom Mill and the beautiful stonework of the Butterley Reservoir spillway in the valley below. Carrying on along the trail by the stone-built Deer Hill Conduit and bridges one can see the craftsmanship that was used to obtain so much water from the hills to supply the reservoirs and towns of the South Pennines.

The route moves on through a quarry in a shooting area and care should be taken not to enter when the red flags are flying. Eventually the path drops down back into the valley and returns to Meltham via a series of lanes and ways that give a sense of how the land was worked in the nineteenth century.

MELTHAM TO WEST NAB

DISTANCE: 15KM/9.3MILES » **TOTAL ASCENT:** 486M/1,594FT » **START GR:** SE 099106 » **TIME:** ALLOW 5 HOURS
SATNAV: HD9 5NW » **MAP:** OS EXPLORER OL1, PEAK DISTRICT: DARK PEAK AREA, AND OL21, SOUTH PENNINES, 1:25,000
REFRESHMENTS: THE SWAN, MELTHAM » **NAVIGATION:** GOOD NAVIGATION SKILLS REQUIRED.

RUINS OF ISOLATED PENNINE FARM BUILDINGS

06 MELTHAM TO WEST NAB

Directions – Meltham to West Nab

↪ From St Bartholomew's Church in the centre of Meltham walk **south-east** along the B6107 Holmfirth Road and **take the sixth road on the right**, Calmlands Road, opposite the school, heading **south-west**. Where the tarmac road ends by the cemetery gates continue **straight ahead** (south-west) along the walled track heading out via Royd Edge to open moorland, crossing two stiles along the way.

2 As the track drops down to Sun Royd **bear right** over two stiles and follow the wall **south-west** maintaining the same course over fields; pass through two iron gates and a wooden stile to exit on to Wessenden Head Road below Meltham Moor.

3 **Turn left** along and cross the road. Walk for 300m, then turn right on to a footpath just after passing the prominent triangular stone known locally as the Cock Crowing Stone. Follow the footpath from the road past the open access notice and take the stile over the fence and ascend to the Ordnance Survey triangulation pillar at West Nab.

4 Continue straight ahead, walking **west** to the fence line and then follow this **south-east** until you reach a stile. Cross the stile and walk down the moor **south-west** following the line of Leyzing Clough. Keep to the **right-hand** side of the clough until you reach the top path which runs along the side of the Wessenden Valley.

5 **Turn right** to follow the higher path **north-west** down the valley, crossing a foot-bridge, until you reach a steel kissing gate at the beginning of the conduit. **Go through the gate** and follow the wide track that runs parallel to the water course on your right-hand side along Binn Moor and Black Edge. Continue on to Holme Moor until the track reaches a bridge over Deer Hill Conduit.

6 Take care and note the signs warning of shooting activity, **DO NOT** enter if unsure of your safety. If there is **NO RED FLAG** flying indicating that no shooting is taking place **turn right** over the bridge and ascend the hill to the quarry above. The clearly defined footpath winds through the quarry workings then exits through a wall running almost **north–south**. After the wall follow the path **downhill** for 150m until you reach a public footpath.

If the **RED FLAG** is flying indicating shooting is taking place **turn left** and follow the footpath downhill to the B6107. **Turn right** and walk along the road until you reach Holt Head. At the junction with the B6109 **turn right** on to a track. Follow the track to Lingards Moor then **turn left** along the footpath to reach Deer Hill End Road. Turn left along the road to rejoin the main route at 8.

7 **Turn left** along the footpath until you almost reach the wall again, where the footpath swings **north-east** to reach Deer Hill Reservoir; follow the footpath along the water's edge to the dam. Continue straight ahead on a road, walking eastwards. Just after the road curves to the left arrive at a public footpath on the right.

8 **Turn right** and go through a gate on to a footpath. **Fork right** and continue to a gate. Go through the gate then immediately **turn left** through a second gate into a walled lane. Shortly afterwards **turn right** over a stone stile with iron railings to follow Catchwater Drain **south-west** to a small dam. Cross the dam and carry on following the watercourse **south-east**, crossing a farm track, to reach a minor road.

9 **Turn left** and walk along the road. At the next junction **turn left** then after a few meters **turn right** on to a footpath, continuing in the same direction when it becomes a road until it reaches a T-junction. **Turn left** then **turn right** at the next junction to arrive back at St Bartholomew's Church in Meltham.

THE TRIANGULATION PILLAR ON BLACKSTONE EDGE

07 Hollingworth Lake to Blackstone Edge

20km/12.4miles

This walk follows the Pennine watershed between Yorkshire and Lancashire and gives stunning views out to the west coast.

Hollingworth Lake » Rakewood » Windy Hill » Blackstone Edge » Blackstone Edge Reservoir » Utley Edge » Chelburn Moor » Sheep Bank » Hollingworth Lake

Start

Hollingworth Lake Visitor Centre.
GR: SD 940153.

The Walk

Hollingworth Lake was once a thriving tourist destination with hotels and entertainment lining the shores. One of the more unusual attractions was watching Captain Matthew Webb who practised swimming in the lake in preparation for becoming the first man to swim across the English Channel.

The walk rises from the lake shore up Longden End Clough to reach Windy Hill; it is surprising how quiet the landscape is as the route works its way to the summit. The route then turns north to follow the Pennine Way across the M62. This is a unique footpath bridge, the only one of its kind along the national trail. The walker gets a sense of exhilaration and trepidation as the traffic thunders below. After this excitement the route keeps to the Pennine Way, crossing Blackstone Edge along the

Pennine watershed separating Yorkshire and Lancashire. The views from Blackstone Edge across Manchester and Lancashire are expansive and give a sense of the urban growth that has taken place over the centuries.

Eventually the route crosses a Roman road, which was subsequently a packhorse route, at the Aiggin Stone. This clearly defined track connected Manchester with Ikley and the tall stone acted as a waymarker for travellers. The walk continues north to Light Hazzles Edge where the Rain Stone, containing one of Simon Armitage's poems on the Stanza Stones poetry trail, can be found carved into the blackened gritstone. Dropping down Chelburn Moor the route works its way through farmland; at one point I was confronted by a donkey sanctuary and a field full of emus – on the outskirts of Rochdale! The final leg follows the Rochdale Way along wide moorland tracks to return to Hollingworth Lake.

HOLLINGWORTH LAKE TO BLACKSTONE EDGE

DISTANCE: 20KM/12.4MILES » **TOTAL ASCENT:** 552M/1,811FT » **START GR:** SD 940153 » **TIME:** ALLOW 6 HOURS **SATNAV:** OL15 0AQ » **MAP:** OS EXPLORER OL21, SOUTH PENNINES, 1:25,000 » **REFRESHMENTS:** HOLLINGWORTH LAKE VISITOR CENTRE CAFE » **NAVIGATION:** GOOD NAVIGATION SKILLS REQUIRED.

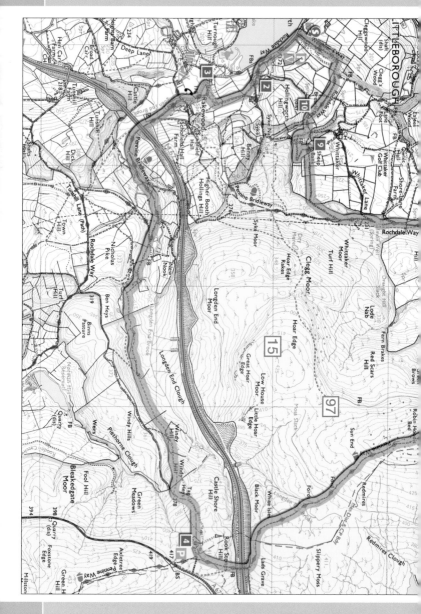

07 HOLLINGWORTH LAKE TO BLACKSTONE EDGE

Directions − Hollingworth Lake to Blackstone Edge

↪ From Hollingworth Lake Visitor Centre walk back to the junction with the minor road skirting Hollingworth Lake. **Turn left** along the road and **bear left** up the cobbled lane.

2 Ignore the first footpath on the right; take the **second narrow footpath on the right**, between a conifer hedge and stone wall at the left of a driveway. Follow the path **south-east** across fields keeping the stone wall to your right, then cross the front of a house and maintain a **south-east** course dropping down into a small valley via a gate. **Turn right** and follow the fence line **south** then **west** through trees to emerge by a stone building. **Turn right** down the short lane to arrive at a minor road.

3 **Turn left** and follow the Pennine Bridleway initially **south-east** under the M62 then generally **east** to reach isolated farm buildings. **Bear right** round the buildings and continue along the bridleway to a wooden gate. Go through the gate and enter Longden End Clough. Keep to the lower path that gently rises up the southern side of the clough walking **east** until you reach the communications mast on the top of Windy Hill.

4 Just after the communications mast **turn left** to take the Pennine Way **north** across the footbridge over the M62. At the northern end of the footbridge by Lads Grave follow the Pennine Way as it curves to the left to head initially **west** then **north-west.** Walk across Blackstone Edge passing the triangulation pillar on your left until you reach a wooden gate and the Peak & Northern Footpath Society signpost at the junction with the Roman road.

5 Go through the gate and **continue straight ahead** then bear left of the Aiggin Stone. Continue on to meet a track running generally north by the side of a conduit. **Turn right** on to this track. Where a bridge crosses the watercourse take the track down to the A58 Halifax Road.

6 **Turn right** and cross over the road, passing The White House pub, then **turn left** to follow the track along Blackstone Edge Reservoir heading **north** for **1.6km**. At a path junction **turn right** over the small stone footbridge across the conduit then **turn left** and follow the footpath to Light Hazzles Edge to view the Rain Stone, part of the Stanza Stones poetry trail.

7 **Retrace your steps** to the path junction by the footbridge; cross over the footbridge and continue straight ahead to descend **westwards** along the footpath on Chelburn Moor until you meet a track running directly **south**. Follow this to Higher Chelburn Reservoir. Where the track splits take the **left hand** fork uphill on to Leach Hill. Go through the gate and follow the Pennine Bridleway **south** crossing Castle Clough until you arrive at the A58 Halifax Road.

8 Cross the road and go through the gate opposite to continue along the Pennine Bridleway around Stormer Hill to a minor road. **Turn right** along the road then shortly afterwards **turn left** on to the Pennine Bridleway and walk for **900m** until you reach a path junction. **Fork right**, leaving the Pennine Bridleway, down to the wall boundary and follow the footpath across fields to Sheep Bank.

9 After passing through the farm buildings **turn left** down the track to reach a stile on the **right** just after a farm gate. **Cross the stile** and follow the track along the embankment **north** to woodland. Do not enter the wood but **turn left** down the field to cross a stream. Ascend the opposite bank then follow the public footpath through the grounds of a private house to exit the property by the driveway on to the Rochdale Way.

10 **Turn right** to follow the Rochdale Way through woodland to return to Hollingworth Lake Visitor Centre.

THE AIGGIN STONE

DERELICT PENNINE FARM ABOVE RYBURN RESERVOIR

08 **Ripponden to Dog Hill**

12.5km/7.8miles

This pleasant walk through the typical landscape and communities of the South Pennines is further enhanced by an old pub.

Ripponden » Rishworth » Pike Law » Blackwood Edge » Dog Hill » Cat Stones » Cat Moss » Grey Stone Height » Ryburn Reservoir » Ripponden

Start
The Old Bridge Inn, Ripponden.
GR: SE 040198.

The Walk
This walk starts and ends at The Old Bridge Inn in Ripponden – it claims to be probably Yorkshire's oldest pub. The route initially follows the River Ryburn up a narrow valley that used to echo to the sound of watermills; the river tumbling over old weirs makes for a pleasant start to the walk.

Once out of the valley the walk passes through Rishworth, a typically old Pennine village with a hall and farm buildings. Eventually the walks rises via the Blackwood Edge Road, an old way across the moor, to Dog Hill. This vantage point gives superb views north and south along the Pennine spine. Good navigation is required across Rishworth Moor and to gain the path back to Ripponden having passed the Cat Stones.

The return route passes through farmland, river valleys and local communities before following the River Ryburn back to Ripponden. The walk back illustrates the thriving communities of the South Pennines where the repurposing and refurbishment of old disused mills into residential spaces has added a vibrancy to the landscape. This is one of the great features of the area, the fact that it has not been halted in its continuing development. It is not unusual to walk through isolated villages and find old weavers' cottages mingling with a restored mill building and some contemporary architecture. All set in a wonderful landscape of river valleys, green pasture and high moorland and in close proximity to major residential and commercial towns.

RIPPONDEN TO DOG HILL

DISTANCE: 12.5KM/7.8MILES » **TOTAL ASCENT:** 360M/1,181FT » **START GR:** SE 040198 » **TIME:** ALLOW 4 HOURS **SATNAV:** HX6 4DF » **MAP:** OS EXPLORER OL21, SOUTH PENNINES, 1:25,000 » **REFRESHMENTS:** THE OLD BRIDGE INN, RIPPONDEN » **NAVIGATION:** GOOD NAVIGATION SKILLS REQUIRED.

THE TRIANGULATION PILLAR ON DOG HILL

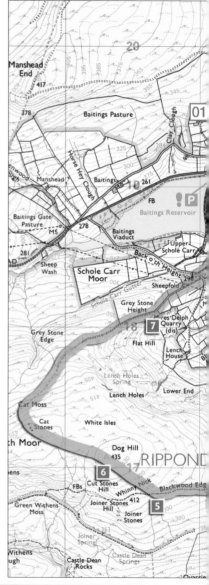

08 **RIPPONDEN TO DOG HILL**

Directions – Ripponden to Dog Hill

↪ From The Old Bridge Inn walk over the stone bridge and **turn right** to reach the B6113 Elland Road. **Turn left** and cross the road then take the first road on the **right** (Mill Fold Way). Follow the road past the car park on the left; the road eventually becomes a riverside trail. Continue walking upstream until steps bring you to a tarmac road. **Turn right** across the bridge then **turn left** along the A672 Oldham Road, crossing to the opposite side.

2 Take the first road on the **right** (Shaw Lane), ascending to stone steps leading on to a field. Go **south-west** across the fields to Rishworth Hall. Walk between the hall and farm buildings to a minor road. **Turn right** along the road then **turn left** on to the footpath between a fence and a wall just after a minor junction. Follow the path **south** to a small signpost then veer **south-west** to a small stream by a hedge. **Cross the stream** and go through the gate and continue on to arrive at a junction with a farm track at Arkin Royd.

3 **Turn right** to walk **west** along the track then over a wooden stile to cross a field and exit via a farm gate on to a tarmac drive. Proceed along the drive and out on to a minor road. **Turn right** along the road then walk for 150m until the road curves to the right at Pike Law and you reach a fingerpost.

4 **Turn left** by the fingerpost. Follow the footpath signs through the garden to a hollow way with a permissive path rising up on to the moor below Pike End. Continue along the path for 700m then go over a ladder stile on to Blackwood Edge. Follow the Blackwood Edge Road (Path) for 1,400m.

5 **Bear north-west** up Whinny Nick to arrive at the Ordnance Survey triangulation pillar on Dog Hill.

6 **Walk north-west** across open moorland to Cat Stones. Then follow the faint path virtually **north** down the hillside to a permissive path indicated by short waymarker posts. Follow the path **north-east** across open moorland eventually arriving at a walled lane at Grey Stone Height.

7 Follow the lane **north-east** to a minor road. **Turn left** along the road then take the first lane on the **right** to walk along the front of houses at Higher Wormald. After the last house **turn right** then **turn left** to walk down a walled lane to reach some ruins.

8 At the ruins follow the fingerpost sign and **turn right** up and slope and through a gate in a wall then **turn left** and follow the footpath **east**, eventually dropping down via a gate through woodland to Ryburn Reservoir.

9 Cross Hutch Brook via the footbridge and follow the footpath through Ryburn Woods then across the dam of Ryburn Reservoir. At the other side of the dam **turn immediately right** and take the footpath that runs along the northern side of the River Ryburn to reach the A672. **Turn right** then cross the road and retrace your steps back to The Old Bridge Inn at Ripponden by the riverside path.

STOODLEY PIKE AND AN APPROACHING STORM FROM DOG HILL

09 **Bride Stones to Mankinholes** 16.3km/10.1miles

Old packhorse routes and strange weathered gritstone formations make this a walk full of history and geology.

Todmorden » Hole Bottom » Bride Stones Moor » Rodwell End » Middle Stoodley House » Stoodley Pike » Mankinholes » Lumbutts » Todmordern

Start
Todmorden Bus Station. GR: SD 937243.

The Walk
The Pennine mill town of Todmorden is worth exploring. Todmorden sits on the edge of Lancashire and Yorkshire and was an important crossing point in the past. The neoclassical town hall sits at the centre and is striking in its juxtaposition with the surrounding buildings. The town is now ascendant again after many decades of decline through the loss of traditional industry.

The walk ascends on to the moors above the town using ancient packhorse routes that were used to cross the area. The views along the valley to the western Pennines are magnificent. The moors are home to the Bride Stones, a series of large gritstone boulders formed into seemingly impossible shapes by the elements. Bride Stones Moor is a good point for panoramic photos of the Calder Valley and surrounding landscape.

The former Poet Laureate Ted Hughes was born in the valley and drew much inspiration from the landscape.

From Bride Stones Moor the route passes by Higher Ashes Farm, a seventeenth-century farmhouse common in these parts. Some of the drystone walls that line the routes are hundreds of years old and stem from successive enclosures of common land. Once the Calder Valley has been crossed the walk ascends to Stoodley Pike and the monument to commemorate the defeat of Napoleon and the surrender of Paris. Steps within the monument lead to a viewing platform. Following the oddly named London Road to the west the walk then passes through Mankinholes, a wonderful little hamlet with a superb water trough and one of the most famous Youth Hostels on the Pennine Way. Then on to Lumbutts and the possibility of lunch at The Top Brink Inn before descending down the valley to return to Todmorden.

BRIDE STONES TO MANKINHOLES
DISTANCE: 16.3KM/10.1MILES » **TOTAL ASCENT:** 679M/2,228FT » **START GR:** SD 937243 » **TIME:** ALLOW 5.5 HOURS
SATNAV: OL14 5DJ » **MAP:** OS EXPLORER OL21, SOUTH PENNINES, 1:25,000 » **REFRESHMENTS:** HARE & HOUNDS, TODMORDEN; THE TOP BRINK INN, LUMBUTTS » **NAVIGATION:** GOOD NAVIGATION SKILLS REQUIRED.

THE BRIDE STONES

09 **BRIDE STONES
TO MANKINHOLES**

Directions – Bride Stones to Mankinholes

⮑ Starting from the bus station in Todmorden walk down Stansfield Road and on to Railway Street. At the junction with Victoria Road **turn right**, go under the railway bridge and take the **second road on the left** (Meadow Bottom Road) uphill to Hole Bottom. Where the road splits take the **left-hand fork** and at the next split take the **right-hand fork** on to a concrete track. **Keep left** at the next fork on to the Calderdale Way and walk by the tops of trees looking down on to Todmorden. Follow the trail as it curves to the **left** to a gate above East Whirlaw Farm.

2 Follow the old packhorse route initially **west** then **north-west** for 1.1km; the route becomes paved with stone and enters a walled lane in later sections. **Fork right** near a derelict barn, as the lane becomes wider and begins to rise. Take the next footpath on the **right**, through the wall, and ascend the moor at Golden Stones. **Bear right** by the buildings at Bride Stones to reach the gritstone outcrop of Great Bride Stones and an Ordnance Survey triangulation pillar.

3 From the triangulation pillar follow the footpath **east** to Eastwood Road. **Turn right** along the road and walk for **400m** then **turn right** along the track. At the farm gate **turn left** then **turn right** and follow the path **south-east** across fields to a minor road.

4 **Turn left** and walk along the road; just after passing Lower Winsley Farm **bear right** and follow the hollow way. Where the hollow way opens out at the junction of four paths **turn right** over a stile and follow the wall line downhill until you reach a path junction just before a gate.

5 **Bear right**, over a stile, and follow the footpath across fields to a walled track. Cross the track and walk through an old quarry to reach another hollow way.

6 **Turn left** along the hollow way passing through Ing Top Barn and on to Higher Ashes Farm, **keeping left** to pass Lower Ashes Farm until you reach a minor road. **Turn left** along the minor road then **turn right** along Matthew Lane, a concrete track. Stay on the concrete track until you reach Rodwell End then follow the track **east** through woodland eventually arriving below the railway line. **Turn right** to go under the railway bridge and arrive at the A646.

7   **Turn left** along the A646, cross the road and **turn right** at the next junction. Follow the bridleway across the Rochdale Canal and uphill to a T-junction. **Turn right** towards Middle Stoodley House, but before reaching it **turn left** along the footpath and ascend fields to reach the Pennine Bridleway below Stoodley Pike.

8   **Turn right** and walk for 300m then **turn left** along the footpath up the hill to the monument. From Stoodley Pike walk **south** along the edge for 500m then take the path on the **right** down the hillside to rejoin the Pennine Bridleway. **Turn left** and follow the trail to a minor road. **Turn right** and walk in to Mankinholes.

9   After passing YHA Mankinholes on the right, **turn left** along the footpath across fields and exit into the pub car park at Lumbutts. Go **right** to reach the footpath on the **left** that delivers you on to the road through the village. Walk along the road for 630m then **turn right** to follow the Calderdale Way through Croft Farm to arrive at a path junction.

10   **Bear left** and cross fields to reach farm buildings. Follow the footpath signs around to the **left** of the farm then descend fields to a housing estate. Follow the footpath signs through the estate as the route winds down the hill eventually bringing you out on to a road. Go straight across and down the steps to the canal. **Turn left** to reach the main road then **turn right** over the canal bridge to the A646 and a return to the bus station in Todmorden.

STOODLEY PIKE FROM ACROSS THE CALDER VALLEY

THE ROAD TO WINTER HILL

10 **Rivington Pike and Winter Hill**   8.6km/5.3miles

A walk that is full of strange buildings, atmospheric landscapes and tantalising views of the west Lancashire coast.

Rivington » Rivington Pike » Crooked Edge Hill » Winter Hill » Noon Hill Slack » Catter Nab » Rivington

Start
Pigeon Tower car park, Rivington.
GR: SD 638148.

The Walk
The walk begins at Rivington Terraced Gardens, built by Lord Leverhulme, the founder of the Lever Brothers soap empire. The gardens and buildings are currently being restored to their former glory by a Rivington Heritage Trust. Within the gardens are wide walks, terraces and pools along with an assortment of unusual buildings including the tall and slender Pigeon Tower.

Next the walk passes Rivington Pike Tower, a short squat tower on Rivington Pike and perhaps one of the most well-known structures in the area. It is situated on the site of a former beacon and has extensive views out to Liverpool Bay and south to Snowdonia. In fine weather it can get very busy but just a short distance away are open moors and tranquillity.

Winter Hill overlooks the towns of Lancashire and is festooned with communication masts. On a clear day Blackpool Tower and Jodrell Bank can be seen. Winter Hill is the site of several tragedies. The first is the murder of a young Scotsman, George Henderson, who was travelling over the moor; an iron post on the hill gives details of his death. Winter Hill is also the site of several air crashes, the most serious happened in 1958 when thirty-five people were killed when a Bristol Freighter crashed in severe weather.

The walk across the moor from Winter Hill back to Rivington gives some excellent views of Rivington Pike Tower and the southern reaches of the River Mersey beyond.

RIVINGTON PIKE AND WINTER HILL

DISTANCE: 8.6KM/5.3MILES » **ASCENT:** 293M/961FT » **START GR:** SD 638148 » **TIME:** ALLOW 3 HOURS **SATNAV:** BL6 7SD » **MAP:** OS EXPLORER 287, WEST PENNINE MOORS, 1:25,000 » **REFRESHMENTS:** SPRING COTTAGE, RIVINGTON » **NAVIGATION:** REASONABLE NAVIGATION SKILLS REQUIRED.

Directions – Rivington Pike and Winter Hill

➎ From the car park take the wide track **south** passing under the seven arch bridge. **Keep left** where the track splits then at the next junction take the **right-hand** footpath on to the track below Rivington Pike Tower. **Turn left** then **turn right** through a gate and ascend the steps leading to the tower.

2 From Rivington Pike Tower take the track **south** down the steep slope and rejoin the main trail via a gate. **Turn left** and follow the trail **south-east** to Pike Cottage.

3 **Turn left** just after the cottage and take the footpath up the steps then **east** across Crooked Edge Hill for **500m**. Below Two Lads **bear left** and follow the faint footpath **north-east** to Winter Hill. Exit on to the access road to the transmitter station and **turn left** to follow this to reach the masts. Note the plaque on the wall of the building relating to the air crash and the iron stump relating to the murder.

THE SEVEN ARCH BRIDGE AT RIVINGTON

4 Keep following the road to the end then **bear left** along the tarmac to the last transmitter. **Bear right** at the fence, then head **west** to Noon Hill Slack, keeping away from the right-hand slope as you walk across the moor. Drop down the other side of the hill bearing slightly **south–west** across Catter Nab to reach a stile giving access on to a wide track.

5 **Turn left** along the track, passing Pigeon Tower on the right. Just after the tower **bear right** into Rivington Terraced Gardens and follow the paths down through the various features to regain the track back to the car park.

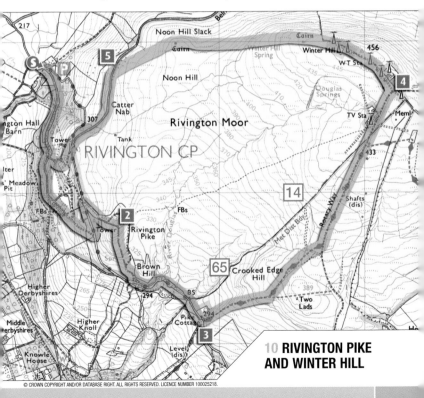

10 RIVINGTON PIKE AND WINTER HILL

© CROWN COPYRIGHT AND/OR DATABASE RIGHT. ALL RIGHTS RESERVED. LICENCE NUMBER 100025218.

SECTION 2

The Northern Walks

The northern walks are characterised by their connection to community, art and literature. It is not surprising given that the Hebden Bridge area is home to a community of artists and their work has permeated across the landscape.

The walks in the north have the big skies of the moors and the wonderful wooded valleys that bisect the area. Spring and autumn are perfect times to visit the area.

The outliers of walks 15 and 17 have been included. Walk 15 includes a climb up Pendle Hill – the guidebook would not be complete without it as the hill is evident in the distance on many of the walks and just asks to be climbed. Walk 17 has been included because of the Singing Ringing Tree – a sculpture that sits above Bury and sings when the wind blows; it is an amazing work of art.

The good rail links across the area also mean that walks can be combined to make for long weekends of exploration.

THE BECK STONE IN BACKSTONE BECK

THE ROCHDALE CANAL AT HEBDEN BRIDGE

11 Hebden Bridge to Stoodley Pike 22.1km/13.7miles

Hebden Bridge station feels like a set from an Agatha Christie movie and perhaps sets the tone for a wonderful walk in this literary landscape.

Hebden Bridge » Heptonstall » Colden Clough » Blackshaw Head » Stoodley Pike » Cragg Vale » Bell House Moor » Hebden Bridge

Start

Hebden Bridge Station. GR: SD 995268.

The Walk

This is a wonderful walk with so much to see it is difficult to decide what is the best bit. The walk starts at Hebden Bridge Station – a delight in itself as it seems like stepping back in time. The route follows the canal towpath out of the town to Mytholm where it begins its climb to Heptonstall and one of the most amazing churches you will ever visit. The graveyard is the resting place of 'King' David Hartley, one of the Cragg Vale Coiners. The coiners clipped the edges off gold coins to make slightly smaller ones, using the clippings to make new coins; their activities are said to have almost brought down the economy in the eighteenth century. The coiners were eventually caught and hanged at York. The graveyard is also the resting place of poet Sylvia Plath, who was married to the Poet Laureate Ted Hughes who was born in nearby Mytholmroyd.

The walk then works its way across a hill via two wonderful cloughs – steep narrow valleys that are encased in woodland. The sound of water tumbling over the gritstone floor makes for a very atmospheric experience. Dean Delph is a surprise as is the high waterfall that cascades off the hill and into the ruins of the old mill. From there the walk crosses the Calder Valley and rises up to the imposing monument of Stoodley Pike. This giant obelisk can be seen for miles across the South Pennines, in fact its presence features in many of the walks in this guidebook even at a significant distance. It is possible to ascend to the viewing balcony for impressive views across the landscape.

From the monument the route descends into Cragg Vale and a very nice pub. Cragg Vale is famous for the coining operation that operated in these parts in the eighteenth century. Leaving Cragg Vale the route crosses the moors, passing the home of 'King' David Hartley at Bell House Moor, before descending again to Hebden Bridge.

HEBDEN BRIDGE TO STOODLEY PIKE

DISTANCE: 22.1KM/13.7MILES » **TOTAL ASCENT:** 877M/2,877FT » **START GR:** SD 995268 » **TIME:** ALLOW 7.5 HOURS
SATNAV: HX7 6JE » **MAP:** OS EXPLORER OL21, SOUTH PENNINES, 1:25,000 » **REFRESHMENTS:** SHOULDER OF MUTTON, HEBDEN BRIDGE; THE HINCHLIFFE ARMS, CRAGG VALE » **NAVIGATION:** GOOD NAVIGATION SKILLS REQUIRED.

STOODLEY PIKE

11 HEBDEN BRIDGE TO STOODLEY PIKE

Directions – Hebden Bridge to Stoodley Pike

➎ From Hebden Bridge Station walk down Station Road and cross the bridge then immediately **turn left** on to the footpath into Calder Holmes Park. Keep to the **right-hand** path and follow the **Rochdale Canal towpath** west to cross over canal bridge number 17 at Black Pit Lock. Continue **west** along the towpath. Shortly after passing a mile post **turn right** on to a footpath to the A646. Cross the road diagonally right and take the footpath between the rear of a house and a road sign.

2 Walk for 50m then **turn right** up a steep wooded slope. At a junction of four paths **turn left** continuing uphill with views over Mytholm. At the next path junction **turn right** and on reaching a wall follow it to the **left** past allotments. **Keep left** at the recreation ground and follow the track across a minor road to the church and ruins at Heptonstall.

3 Retrace your steps to the minor road and follow the concrete track **south-west** to Eaves Wood. **Turn right** on the footpath along the top of the woods to exit on to a minor road. **Turn left** along the road; the road becomes a track. Descend Lumb Bank arriving at cobble stones leading to a stone bridge at the bottom of Colden Clough.

4 Go over the bridge and **turn left** along a wide track. **After 150m turn sharp right** uphill; walk for **1,500m** to reach Shaw Bottom. **Turn left** at the junction and walk up the short road, carrying straight on into a walled lane. Take the first footpath on the **right** through a gate heading **south-west** over a series of stiles to a road at Blackshaw Head. **Turn right then immediately left** following the public footpath between houses and across fields to Lower Blackshaw Farm. Keep to the **left** of the buildings and continue directly south to reach Hippins.

5 **Turn left** through a gate and follow the wall line to a signpost. Take the unmarked footpath **south-east** down to a footbridge and cross the stream. **Turn left** and follow the path downstream, taking the **left-hand** branch where it forks eventually to exit on to a concrete farm track. Follow the track down across the stream then head **north-east** to Higher Underbank Farm, **keeping right** where the track splits. Follow the public footpath **right**, through the farm and down the hillside to arrive at houses and workshops by the stream. **Turn left** along the lane under the railway bridge to reach the A646. **Turn left** along the road then cross over to take the next junction on the **right**.

6 Cross the canal bridge and **turn right** along the footpath (Callis Wood Bottom). Walk in front of the houses and enter woodland via a wooden stile secreted in the hedge at the very end. Ascend to Oaks Farm. **Bear left** to maintain an upward course past the derelict farm building at Thorps, finally reaching a defined grassy track contouring Lodge Hill above the hamlet of Higham. As the landscape flattens out go over the stile and follow the Pennine Way uphill crossing the Pennine Bridleway. At the top go through the gate and **turn right** to arrive at Stoodley Pike.

7 Head directly **south** from the monument along the permissive path and cross a stone wall via the ladder stile. Continue following the footpath down Higher Moor to meet the track by Withens Clough Reservoir. **Turn left** and proceed along the Calderdale Way to Cragg Vale.

8 Take the footpath to the immediate **right** of The Hinchliffe Arms in Cragg Vale going through woodland; keep to the public footpath where it passes through private property. Where the path becomes a tarmac lane **keep left** at the forks and zigzag up the hillside to Upper Lumb. Follow the stone track between buildings to a hollow way that rises to open pasture. Go through the field gate and continue following the hollow way up to a wide vehicle track at High Green.

9 **Turn right** along the track initially heading **north-east** then **north-west** across Bell House Moor, passing above Bell House. At the head of Broadhead Clough take the path heading **north-east** across Erringden Moor to a wall corner at Broad Head.

10 Follow the fingerpost **east** along the wall line into a walled lane. Where lanes cross **turn left** then **turn right** along the next footpath heading down through fields to the hamlet of Park. **Turn left** along Park Lane, which becomes Wood Hey Lane until you reach Spencer Lane. **Turn right** and follow the concrete lane through Wood Top back to Hebden Bridge Station.

THE ABANDONED FARMHOUSE AT RAISTRICK GREAVE

12 **Hardcastle Crags**

15.8km/9.8miles

Walk this route in autumn when the leaf has fallen and covered the floor of Hebden Dale in the golden emblem of woodland.

New Bridge » Slack » Standing Stone Hill » Reaps Cross » Ridge Scout » Hardcastle Crags » New Bridge

Start

National Trust Midgehole car park (parking charge), New Bridge. GR: SD 988291.

The Walk

This is grouse shooting country and open access should be assessed before setting off on the walk. For the best experience walk this route in autumn to gain the full effect of golden leaves and earthy smells of the woodlands in Hebden Dale.

The walk starts from New Bridge at the bottom of Hebden Dale and ascends through beech and oak woodlands to small Pennine communities before heading out on to the moors. The first half of the route follows old ways across the Pennines, the stone marker at Reaps Cross denoting a medieval trail. The views across the moors and down the valleys are extensive and the ruined farmhouse at Raistrick Greave is very atmospheric. Perhaps this is due to the history of this part of Calderdale during the Civil War when a battle was fought around Heptonstall between the Royalists and Parliamentarian forces.

The walk down to Hebden Dale from Gorple Lower Reservoir follows Graining Water downstream as it cuts its way in to the gritstone rock. The footpath gives a high-level view of this narrow gorge and along the way the walker may come across boulder athletes honing their skills on the rock. Once past Black Dean the route begins to enter the woodlands that surround Hardcastle Crags. In autumn the ground and sky are filled with the golden hues of nature going to sleep before the coming winter, making for a pleasing experience. Hardcastle Crags can be easily missed off the forest trail so keep your eyes open for the path leading to it on the right. The view from the top of the crag along Hebden Dale is a good vantage point for birdwatching. Shortly after the trails passes Gibson Mill and a welcome break in the National Trust cafe before returning to New Bridge.

HARDCASTLE CRAGS

DISTANCE: 15.8KM/9.8MILES » **TOTAL ASCENT:** 381M/1,250FT » **START GR:** SD 988291 » **TIME:** ALLOW 5 HOURS **SATNAV:** HX7 7AA » **MAP:** OS EXPLORER OL21, SOUTH PENNINES, 1:25,000 » **REFRESHMENTS:** WEAVING SHED CAFE, GIBSON MILL » **NAVIGATION:** GOOD NAVIGATION SKILLS REQUIRED.

WASHDAY ON THE MOOR AT POPPLES

12 HARDCASTLE CRAGS

Directions – Hardcastle Crags

⊙→ From Midgehole car park **turn left** and walk along the road and **turn right** to go across Hebden Water. On the opposite bank take the footpath to the **right** of a house up through woodland. Where the path intersects another go straight across and continue up, exiting via a flight of stone steps into open land.

2 **Turn right,** crossing a stile, and walk for **700m** then **turn left** along a walled lane to exit on to the road at Slack. **Turn right,** keeping **left** at the fork in the road and take the next footpath on the **left**. Follow the footpath across the area known as Popples to eventually cross the road on to a farm track. After 100m **turn left** and follow the farm track heading **west**, keeping **left** where it splits to arrive at a gate giving access on to the moor.

3 Follow the wall line **north-west** and at the corner of the wall maintain course across Black Mires passing the Standing Stone along the way to reach the Ordnance Survey triangulation pillar on Standing Stone Hill.

4 Go **west** across open moorland to Reaps Cross; continue in the same direction for a further **600m** then follow the footpath north-west across Heptonstall Moor to arrive at the abandoned farmhouse at Raistrick Greave.

5 Follow the footpath **north-west** through the ruins to reach the footpath running down the **eastern** side of Clegg Foot. Continue walking downstream and cross the footbridge over Reaps Water then ascend the opposite bank going over the stile on to the concrete track in front of the shooting cabin.

6 **Turn right** and follow the track downhill to Gorple Lower Reservoir. **Turn right** across the dam; **turn left** at the other end of the dam and **turn left** again to descend to the footbridge over Graining Water. Cross the bridge and **turn right** up the steep bank to reach Ridge Scout. Walk **east** past gritstone outcrops to reach a minor road.

7 **Turn right** to follow the road downhill; at the first bend **turn left** and go through a gate on to a wide track. After 70m **turn right** through a gate and down steps. Cross the footbridge across Alcomden Water and ascend the opposite bank. Walk along the waymarked footpath **east** across Black Dean eventually descending through fields to Over Wood.

8 Take the track along the front of the house and enter woodland. Follow the woodland trail for **1.4km** to Hardcastle Crags. **Turn right** to reach the top of the crag and enjoy the views. Retrace your steps back to the trail and **turn right** to reach the visitor centre at Gibson Mill.

9 From the visitor centre regain the trail and continue **south-east** through Hebden Dale to arrive back at Midgehole car park.

HARDCASTLE CRAGS

AN OLD HEDGE LINE ABOVE THE BRONTË BRIDGE

13 Haworth to Top Withens

13.5km/8.4miles

A walk to one of the most famous ruins in literature. This gentle walk is difficult to complete without humming along to Kate Bush's hit 'Wuthering Heights'.

Haworth » Penistone Hill » Haworth Moor » Oxenhope Stoop Hill » Top Withens » Brontë Bridge » Haworth

Start

Haworth Church. GR: SE 030372.

The Walk

This is grouse shooting country and open access should be assessed before setting off on the walk. This is a relatively gentle walk along well-made trails, with just the section to Oxenhope Stoop Hill from the track that can prove a little taxing. Combined with the historical aspects of the area it makes for a day out packed with possibilities.

The beginning is a step back in time. Starting from the church in the village of Haworth with its cobbled streets and plentiful shops. This is the home of the famous Brontë family; the Brontë Parsonage Museum sits behind the church and is worth a visit to see how the family lived and wrote such wonderful prose. Leaving Haworth, the route follows well-made trails across Penistone Hill then heads out on to Haworth Moor along a wide track.

Just before reaching Harbour Lodge the route follows a public footpath up a steep hillside to arrive at Oxenhope Stoop Hill. This position gives superb views across the South Pennine hills. Listen out for the whistle and puff of steam trains running along the Keighley and Worth Valley Railway nearby.

From this point the walk follows a series of waymarkers across the moor to join the Pennine Way below Dick Delf Hill. Turning north you soon find Top Withens, said to be the inspiration for a location in Emily Brontë's novel *Wuthering Heights*. The site is always busy with visitors. From there the walk heads east dropping down to a narrow valley where the Brontë Waterfalls and Brontë Bridge are situated. The route then ascends to Penistone Hill and onwards back to Haworth. The village has many facilities from teashops and pubs to shops selling items of interest to Brontë followers.

HAWORTH TO TOP WITHENS

DISTANCE: 13.5KM/8.4MILES » **TOTAL ASCENT:** 318M/1,043FT » **START GR:** SE 030372 » **TIME:** ALLOW 4 HOURS
SATNAV: BD22 8DR » **MAP:** OS EXPLORER OL21, SOUTH PENNINES, 1:25,000 » **REFRESHMENTS:** BLACK BULL, HAWORTH
NAVIGATION: GOOD NAVIGATION SKILLS REQUIRED.

Directions — Haworth to Top Withens

➎ Take the footpath between the Black Bull pub and Haworth Church heading **south-west** to a path junction. **Turn right** to follow the fingerpost pointing the way to *Top Withens*. Cross the road and enter Penistone Hill Country Park.

2 Walk **south-west** past the Ordnance Survey triangulation pillar and the old quarry workings. On reaching the wall go **right** and follow the track, keeping **left** where the track splits, to reach the road. **Turn left** and cross over the road; walk until you reach a track on the right.

3 **Turn right** on to the track on Yorkshire Water land; follow the track west for **2.1km** to the foot of Round Hill.

4 **Turn left** on to the public footpath across Wether Hill to Spa Hill Clough. Cross the stream and ascend the hillside **south-west** to reach Oxenhope Stoop Hill.

5 Follow the short marker posts and boundary stones **west** across the moor to Dick Delf Hill and then on to meet the Pennine Way. **Turn right** and follow the Pennine Way **north** to arrive at Top Withens.

6 After visiting the site continue **north-east** along the paved Pennine Way following the wide, well-defined trail to Upper Heights.

7 **Bear right** across The Height towards a tree plantation. At the **north-east** corner of the trees **turn right** along a footpath through the gate and follow it **south** downhill to reach Brontë Bridge. Cross the bridge and **turn left** following the flow of water downstream. The path begins to rise up the hillside to arrive at Middle Intake Farm.

8 **Bear right** along the track ascending on to the moor along the Millennium Way. Cross the road to the car park and retrace your steps across Penistone Hill back to Haworth.

**13 HAWORTH
TO TOP WITHENS**

14 Wycoller to Great Wolf Stones

16km/9.9miles

The beautiful village of Wycoller makes a great base to explore the moors above Colne. After visiting Great Wolf Stones, the walk returns via the second Pennine Panopticon, The Atom.

Wycoller » Watersheddles Reservoir » Silver Hill » Slippery Stones Farm » Great Wolf Stones » The Atom » Wycoller

Start

Wycoller Country Park car park (parking charge). GR: SD 926395.

The Walk

Wycoller, on the outskirts of the Lancashire town of Colne, was once a weaving community that fell on hard times during the cotton mill boom that spread across the north-west of England. The weavers were forced to move into the towns for work and their looms and cottages fell silent. The village has strong connections with Charlotte Brontë, who is thought to have based Ferndean Manor in *Jane Eyre* on Wycoller Hall. She would pass through the village on her way from Haworth to visit friends and would have known the building well. Sadly, the hall is no more – a victim of gambling and debt. After the death of the last owner the stone was plundered for housing and the hall fell into ruin. The village has a wonderful clapper bridge and a packhorse bridge; a little further downstream there is a bridge made from an iron age menhir. The area is now a country park and a pleasant place to spend time watching birds or simply enjoying tea and cake in the tearoom.

The walk follows the Wycoller Beck downstream, passing by Watersheddles Reservoir where the route joins a deep clough with the River Worth tumbling down the gritstone bedrock. It then heads north on to the moors to Great Wolf Stones, a gritstone outcrop overlooking the former cotton towns of Lancashire. Good navigation is then required to negotiate a short walk across open moor to reach the old hollow way that heads south-west towards Wycoller.

Before reaching the village, the walk passes The Atom, one of the Pennine Panopticons. On the return into Wycoller look out for the strange vertical stones called orthostats that form boundaries along the ancient lanes.

WYCOLLER TO GREAT WOLF STONES

DISTANCE: 16KM/9.9MILES » **TOTAL ASCENT:** 393M/1,289FT » **START GR:** SD 926395 » **TIME:** ALLOW 5 HOURS
SATNAV: BB8 8SY » **MAP:** OS EXPLORER OL21, SOUTH PENNINES, 1:25,000 » **REFRESHMENTS:** WYCOLLER CRAFT CENTRE AND TEAROOMS » **NAVIGATION:** GOOD NAVIGATION SKILLS REQUIRED.

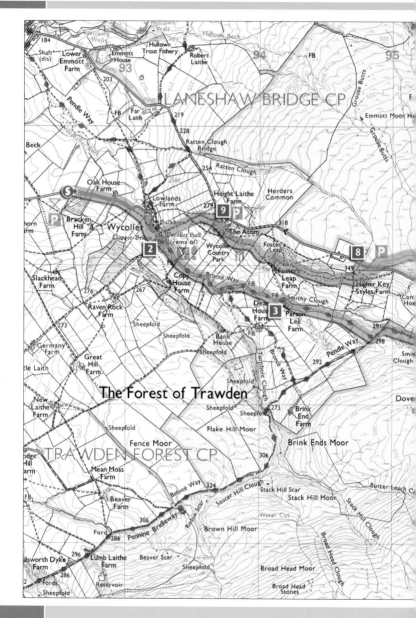

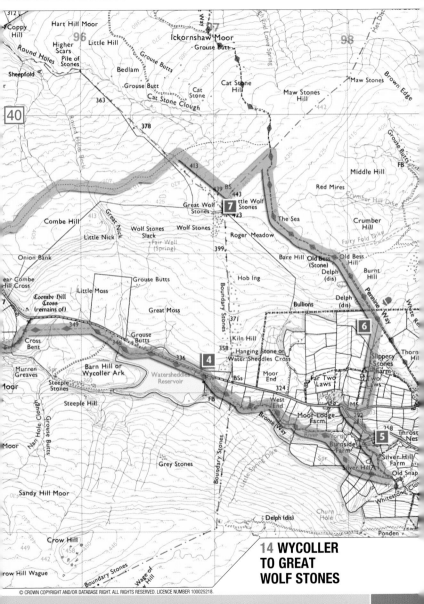

14 WYCOLLER TO GREAT WOLF STONES

Directions – Wycoller to Great Wolf Stones

❻ Head **south-east** out of the car park and follow the footpath along the side of the road until the road turns sharp left. Go **straight ahead** over the stile and walk across the fields until you reach a tarmac lane. **Turn left** along the lane and walk into centre of Wycoller.

2 Cross Wycoller Beck by the packhorse bridge then **turn right** in front of the remains of Wycoller Hall and follow Wycoller Beck downstream in the direction of the signposted Thursden Valley.

3 **Bear left** at Parson Lee Farm and follow the waymark posts to a concrete farm track. **Turn left** down the hill and follow the track until a gate on the **right** gives access to a concessionary path which takes you through Cross Bent to Watersheddles Reservoir. Follow the path over the ladder stile and around the northern edge of the water.

4 On reaching the dam go to the **right** of the shooting cabin and take the footpath along the River Worth, crossing the county boundary. After **630m** cross a footbridge and walk up the opposite bank to Silver Hill. **Turn left** and follow the walled lane **east** down to Old Snap then turn **sharp left** to descend **north-west** to go through Silver Hill Farm. Follow the footpath along the tarmac lane to the junction with a minor road.

5 **Turn left** along the road and **turn right** at the next junction. Walk along the road then take the **second footpath on the left.** Walk through Slippery Stones Farm **bearing left then right** around the farm building to enter a walled lane heading **north**. Continue uphill until the Pennine Way is reached by a wall running north-west.

6 **Turn left** along the Pennine Way heading **north-west** and walk for **1.6km**. Leave the Pennine Way and walk **south-west** across open moorland for **400m** to reach the Ordnance Survey triangulation pillar on Great Wolf Stones.

7 Walk **north-west** across open moorland for **500m** using a stile at an access point to overcome the wire fence and reach the hollow way. **Turn left** heading **south-west** and follow the ancient depression to a stile by the corner of a fence and wall. Exit on to the road and **turn left** before crossing the road to reach the public footpath opposite.

8 Follow the footpath down to Higher Key Styles Farm then **turn right** heading **west** to walk along the front of the farm buildings and exit on to rough moorland via a small gate. Continue heading **west** until a tarmac track is reached leading to Fosters Leap Farm. **Turn left** along the track then where the track turns sharp left go **straight ahead** to a gate giving access to fields. Cross the field bearing **right** uphill and exit via a gate to follow the path across the hillside to arrive at The Atom.

9 Take the footpath **north-west** from the viewpoint and descend the walled lane back into Wycoller. Cross the Wycoller Beck and **turn right** through the village to follow the lane back to the car park.

SCOUT ON THE TRIANGULATION PILLAR AT GREAT WOLF STONES

OGDEN CLOUGH

15 Barley to Pendle Hill

7.7km/4.8miles

The pretty little village of Barley sits below the hulking presence of Pendle Hill and makes for a great base from which to make your ascent to Big End.

Barley » Ogden Clough » Boar Clough » Big End » Pendle Way » Barley

Start

Barley car park (parking charge).
GR: SD 823403.

The Walk

This walk is relatively short and the ascent not too onerous. It would make a perfect winter walk on a bright day with blue skies and snow on the ground. Or for a summer solstice to watch the setting sun.

A local saying states that 'If you can see Pendle Hill then it is going to rain. If you cannot see it then it is already raining.' Pendle derives from the Celtic word 'penn', meaning 'hill', so this is literally 'hill hill'. It is an outlier of the South Pennines, but its presence is visible from many of the hills further east and south, and makes such enticing overtures whenever a walker summits them that it would be remiss to exclude it from any guidebook. The popular route up is from Barley, via the Pendle Way;

on sunny days many people can be seen struggling up the steep face of the hill. This route replaces the steep climb with a nice stroll up Ogden Clough and then on to the summit via the gentle Boar Clough. Watch out for birdlife along this section of the walk including dotterel, black redstart and, in winter, the snow bunting.

The summit is known as 'Big End' and gives expansive views across the Pennines and out to the western coast of Britain. These views had such a profound effect on George Fox that he went on to found the Quaker movement. Markers around the triangulation pillar tell of the most famous period of history in this area; in 1612 ten local people, mainly women, were tried for witchcraft following a series of prior accusations. Nine were found guilty and hanged on Gallows Hill in Lancaster.

BARLEY TO PENDLE HILL

DISTANCE: 7.7KM/4.8MILES » **TOTAL ASCENT:** 354M/1,161FT » **START GR:** SD 823403 » **TIME:** ALLOW 2.5 HOURS
SATNAV: BB12 9JX » **MAP:** OS EXPLORER OL21, SOUTH PENNINES, 1:25,000 » **REFRESHMENTS:** BARLEY MOW, BARLEY
NAVIGATION: REASONABLE NAVIGATION SKILLS REQUIRED.

Directions – Barley to Pendle Hill

6 Exit the car park and **turn right** to reach the junction with the main road. Go straight across **bearing left** to enter the lane passing the village hall and mountain rescue post. Follow the lane along Ogden Clough for 1.8km to reach a gate at the foot of Upper Ogden Reservoir dam.

2 Go through the gate and take the footpath on the **right** up to the top of the dam then follow the wall line along to a second gate; this gives access to the Pendle Way that runs along the northern edge of the reservoir. At a gate leading down to a stream **turn right** and follow the path uphill through Fox Holes then **bear left** to cross the stream in Boar Clough.

3 **Turn right** and ascend the path up the western flank of Boar Clough following a line of cairns to maintain course.

4 After 450m **cross the stream** following the path **north–east** until the path intersects with a wide trail. **Turn left** to arrive at the Ordnance Survey triangulation pillar at Big End.

5 Continue **north** to a wall then **turn right** to follow the wall downhill for 50m. **Turn right** along a wide trail and descend the eastern flank of the hill. At the wall corner follow the wall line downhill then pass through two gates and exit on to a road.

THE PENDLE WAY

6 Take the gate immediately to the **right** of the one just exited and follow the footpath **south-west** across the back of Pendle House. At the end of the buildings **turn left** and take the wide track **south-east**. Go through the gate and maintain course across the field leaving by a steel gate. Follow the path down a hollow way past Brown House then through a wooden gate and across a footbridge to walk through Ings End.

7 Leave Ings End following the lane initially **east** until it sweeps left then take the footpath on the **right** across a footbridge. Cross the field to go through a wooden gate and follow the stream to return to Barley. **Turn right** along the road then just after the Barley Mow pub **turn left** along footpath to return to the car park.

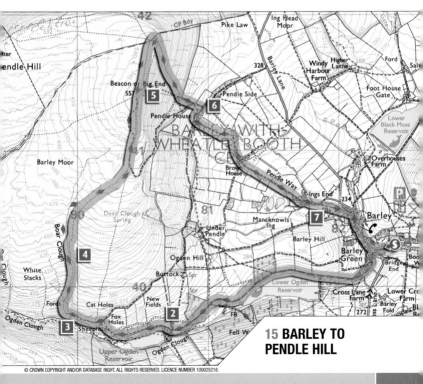

15 BARLEY TO PENDLE HILL

© CROWN COPYRIGHT AND/OR DATABASE RIGHT. ALL RIGHTS RESERVED. LICENCE NUMBER 100025218.

FROST AROUND THURSDEN BROOK

16 **Thursden to Gorple Stones** 12.6km/7.8miles

Thursden Valley is a geologist's delight, being a mixture of Kinder gritstone, shale and limestone brought from Yorkshire by glacier.

Halifax Road » Thursden Valley » Delf Hill » Ben Edge » Gorple Stones » Widdop Reservoir » Extwistle Moor » Thursden » Halifax Road

Start

Car park on Halifax Road,
north of Thursden. GR: SD 901351.

The Walk

This is an excellent walk for historians and geologists. The walk uses well-defined footpaths and bridleways, along with a short section of quiet road. Thursden Valley is a mixture of Kinder gritstone, shale and limestone brought into the valley from Yorkshire by glacial processes as the ice flowed out to the west into what was a German sea. Lead and coal are also present and were extensively mined around the area. Today, in the valley floor we see a mixture of moraine and the evidence of hushing, created when surface material was washed away to reveal the mineral deposits below. Finding large deposits of limestone similar to the rocks of Malham can at first be confusing but, once the events are understood, makes perfect sense.

The area sits astride the boundary of Lancashire and Yorkshire making it an important crossing point in medieval times. The waymarker of Widdop Cross was situated near Widdop Reservoir helping travellers cross these featureless moors; it was destroyed in the mid 1950s. Extwistle Moor was once cultivated land and is a good example of enclosure and change of purpose, initially for sheep rearing and then grouse shooting. In the Middle Ages landowners enclosed common lands and evicted commoners who could be replaced more profitably with sheep.

The gritstone outcrop of the Gorple Stones sits by the Pennine Bridleway offering a chance of some climbing and bouldering with fine views, although the British Mountaineering Council website does carry a warning that the stones are 'dangerously close to the Lancashire Border'. But do not worry – they ARE in Yorkshire.

THURSDEN TO GORPLE STONES

DISTANCE: 12.6KM/7.8MILES » **TOTAL ASCENT:** 464M/1,522FT » **START GR:** GR: SD 901351 » **TIME:** ALLOW 4.5 HOURS
SATNAV: BB10 3RB » **MAP:** OS EXPLORER OL21, SOUTH PENNINES, 1:25,000 » **REFRESHMENTS:** THE VICTORIA INN,
BURNLEY » **NAVIGATION:** SIMPLE NAVIGATION SKILLS REQUIRED.

Directions – Thursden to Gorple Stones

⊙► Cross the stile and walk **south-west** down the field to a minor road. **Turn left** and then take the next public footpath on the **right** past the house at Stephen Hey, exiting via a gate then cross fields to a wooden stile. Go over the stile and through the farm gate on the **right**. **Turn immediately left** and descend the steep bank to cross the footbridge over Thursden Brook.

2 **Turn right** and follow the waymarker signs generally **south-west** through woodland, eventually following a stone wall and later a farm track to the top of the hill and a short marker post. Follow the short marker post to the **south** to reach a ladder stile over a wall then **turn left** uphill, crossing a stile and ascend the slope to a farm gate. **Turn right** and follow the wall line **turning left** at the corner. Note the blocks of limestone laying on the surface of the field. Go through a gate and enter Delf Hill **bearing right** to reach the Ordnance Survey triangulation pillar.

3 Walk directly **south** to reach a gate in the wall at the bottom of the hill. Go **left** through the gate and follow the grassy track **east** to meet the Pennine Bridleway. **Turn right** along the Pennine Bridleway following it **south-west** for **1.5km** exiting via a gate on to the wide track. Note the glacial moraines above Hurstwood Reservoir.

4 Follow the track **east** passing through gate after **1.7km**. Continue **straight ahead** for **1.4km,** passing the Gorple Stones above the track, until you reach a path junction with a signpost on the left.

5 **Turn left** to follow the footpath along the western side of Widdop Reservoir. After passing a series of small dams upstream of the reservoir, ford the stream below Flaught Hill and ascend the opposite bank to a minor road. **Turn left** and walk along the road until you reach the metal barrier blocking access to a track on the right.

6 **Turn left** and follow the faint footpath heading **west** across Extwistle Moor and exit via a gate on to the Pennine Bridleway.

7 **Turn right** to follow the trail **north** to a minor road above New Bridge. **Turn left** along the road and **fork left** immediately afterwards noting the evidence of hushing (an ancient mining method) on the left. Walk for 250m until you reach a driveway on your right.

8 **Turn right** along the driveway and follow the footpath up through woodland to a road. **Turn left** along the road then turn left at the next junction to return to the car park.

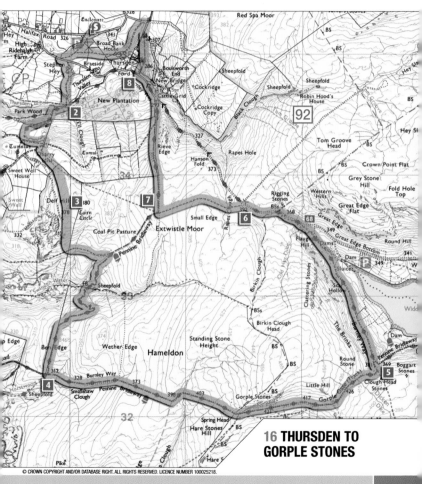

16 THURSDEN TO GORPLE STONES

17 Goodshaw to Hameldon Hill   17.6km/10.9miles

A walk giving excellent views to the west coast. Goodshaw Chapel is an excellent example of a nonconformist chapel while the Singing Ringing Tree is a unique art installation best visited when it is windy.

Goodshaw » Rossendale Way » Singing Ringing Tree » Hameldon Hill » Great Hameldon » Goodshaw

Start

Goodshaw Chapel, Crawshawbooth.
GR: SD 815263.

The Walk

This is a walk of heritage, art, high moorland landscapes and extensive views. The walk starts at Goodshaw Chapel, a superb example of a nonconformist chapel from the eighteenth century. It is worth visiting the interior to see the original box-pews. Access is by arrangement with the key keeper:
www.english-heritage.org.uk/visit/ places/goodshaw-chapel

The chapel sits by what used to be the main road to Burnley and would have serviced remote farmhouses on the moors. This gives an indication how much the landscape has changed in the 200 years since the chapel was built.

The route heads north-east from Goodshaw along easy trails across the moors. The Singing Ringing Tree sits at the most easterly point of the walk. This sound sculpture sings when the wind blows. It is part of the Pennine Panopticons that were erected across East Lancashire as part of the renaissance of the area. The pipes have a range of several octaves and are tuned to give choral harmonics.

Next the walk returns west with excellent views out to the west coast on clear days. The radar weather station on Hameldon Hill gives a slightly eerie feel to the area; its remote location and strange structures bringing up images of other worlds. From there the walk up on to Great Hameldon is worth the effort for the views. From the vantage point of the Ordnance Survey triangulation pillar a panorama of Pendle Hill, Great Whernside and Buckden Pike can be seen in all their glory. The return to Goodshaw is a gentle amble across moorland paths and tracks.

GOODSHAW TO HAMELDON HILL

DISTANCE: 17.6KM/10.9MILES » **TOTAL ASCENT:** 428M/1,404FT » **START GR:** SD 815263 » **TIME:** ALLOW 5.5 HOURS
SATNAV: BB4 8QB » **MAP:** OS EXPLORER OL21, SOUTH PENNINES, AND 287, WEST PENNINE MOORS, 1:25,000
REFRESHMENTS: THE WHITE BULL, GOODSHAW » **NAVIGATION:** GOOD NAVIGATION SKILLS REQUIRED.

17 GOODSHAW TO HAMELDON HILL

Directions – Goodshaw to Hameldon Hill

❺ From Goodshaw Chapel walk **north** along the road and take the second public footpath on the **right**, the Rossendale Way. Follow this **east** for 2.6km until you reach Compston's Cross, that marks the junction of several old packhorse and monastic routes.

2 Do not follow the Rossendale Way. Walk **straight ahead** through a gate and take the track heading **north-east**. After passing through a gate **turn left** over the next stile and follow the concessionary path to Crown Point. Cross the road and follow the trail to the Singing Ringing Tree. Retrace your steps back to the road.

3 **Turn right** and walk for 200m along the road then **turn left** through the gate. Follow the footpath through a break in a stone wall, then follow the wall line generally heading **west** descending to the ruins of a building.

4 **Turn right** to follow the footpath **north** to the entrance to Dunnockshaw Community Woodland. **Turn left** to walk **west** along the edge of the trees and exit on to open moor via a gate. Follow the short marker posts initially **north** then **west** across the moor to exit via a gate on to the A682 at Wholaw Nook.

5 Go straight across the road and follow the Burnley Way **south-west**. Take the first public footpath on the **right**, over the wall, and follow the wall line uphill below powerlines. Keep walking **north-west** crossing the wall then entering a sunken track. Follow the public footpath as it curves **north-east** downhill in the general direction of the wind turbine to a wall.

6 On reaching the wall **turn left** to head **south-west** and follow the footpath uphill to Porters Gate Height. Keep on the same bearing across Black Hill to a ladder stile. Go over the wall and take the public footpath below the weather station on Hameldon Hill. Exit on to a wide track then **turn right** to follow the track **west** past the communications masts. Keep on the track for 700m to reach a gate.

7 Go through the gate and walk **west** for 600m then **north-west** along the natural line of the slope to reach the Ordnance Survey triangulation pillar on Great Hameldon. Take the footpath **south-west** from the pillar to the stone wall. Follow the wall **south-east** for 550m.

8 Take the concessionary path **south** through the gap in the wall towards Mitchell's House Reservoirs. Exit on to the bridleway and **turn left** and follow the wall line all the way to a walled lane. Enter the lane and **turn right** up the sunken path to meet the Rossendale Way.

9 **Turn left** along the Rossendale Way, heading **east** on the faint path across open moorland, then drop down through farmland to a lane skirting ponds. **Turn right** along the lane to reach the rear of houses; **bear left** and **left** again at the next junction. Continue straight ahead to reach the A682.

10 Cross the A682 and take the footpath to the right of the house opposite. Follow the footpath up through farmland and exit on to a minor road by Swinshaw Hall. **Turn right** and walk along the road back to Goodshaw Chapel.

COMPSTON'S CROSS

GRITSTONE OUTCROP ON BURLEY MOOR

18 Burley in Wharfedale to the Twelve Apostles

14km/8.7miles

This beautiful walk is your chance to leave a poem in a postbox hidden on a South Pennine moor.

Burley in Wharfedale » Burley Moor » Horncliffe Well » Twelve Apostles » Backstone Beck » Dales Way » Burley in Wharfedale

Start

Burley in Wharfedale Station.
GR: SE 163458.

The Walk

This is a delight of a walk. Enjoy it on a fine summer day, allowing plenty of time to sit and enjoy the views. Burley in Wharfedale is a beautiful Yorkshire market town, full of interesting shops and cafes; good rail and road access make it a superb base for a weekend of walking.

The relaxing ascent up on to the moors gives time for the views to be taken in. The views are wide and far. The Yorkshire Dales can be seen to the north and the edges of the Lake District to the west. Accompanying such views is a wealth of

historical interest including hidden wells, rock art with cup and ring markings adorning many gritstone boulders, ancient waymarks and posts showing the passages across the moor and time, and the wonderful Twelve Apostles stone circle – probably one of the best in Yorkshire. From the stone circle the white golf balls of the RAF Menwith Hill can be seen – a rather ominous part of the landscape.

The return journey passes by a unique postbox, specifically for your poems, to be enjoyed by all – including the Poet Laureate Simon Armitage. The Poetry Postbox and Poetry Seat are part of the Stanza Stones poetry trail. Remember to take a pencil and paper.

BURLEY IN WHARFEDALE TO THE TWELVE APOSTLES

DISTANCE: 14KM/8.7MILES » **TOTAL ASCENT:** 368M/1,207FT » **START GR:** SE 163458 » **TIME:** ALLOW 4.5 HOURS **SATNAV:** LS29 7AA » **MAP:** OS EXPLORER 297, LOWER WHARFEDALE & WASHBURN VALLEY, 1:25,000 **REFRESHMENTS:** THE RED LION, BURLEY IN WHARFEDALE » **NAVIGATION:** GOOD NAVIGATION SKILLS REQUIRED.

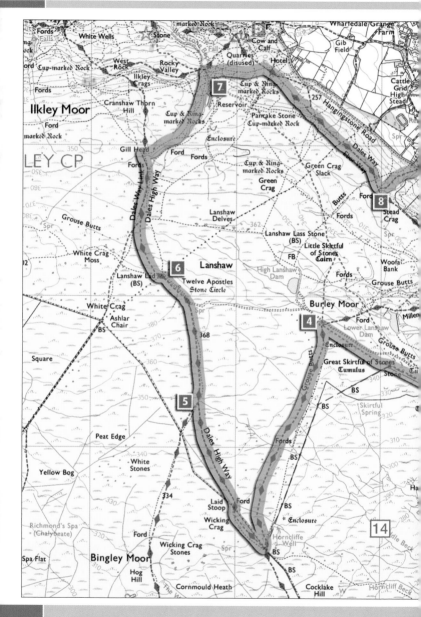

18 BURLEY IN WHARFEDALE TO THE TWELVE APOSTLES

Directions – Burley in Wharfedale to the Twelve Apostles

➲ Exit Burley in Wharfedale Station by the **west** platform and **turn left** into Hag Farm Road. Take the first public footpath on the **right**, through the gate across fields to woodland. Follow the waymarker signs through the woods and across fields to exit on to a small lane. **Turn left** and walk to a road junction. **Turn right** and walk along the road for **60m**.

2 **Turn left** on to the footpath out on to the moor, **bearing left** at the house boundary wall. Follow the wall **south** to a tarmac track then keep to the wall line for **500m** to reach an overhead powerline.

3 **Turn right** up to a stony track with a fence to the left. Go **north-west** passing the Great Skirtful of Stones on the left, then a wooden shooting hut, until reaching a path junction and gritstone outcrop on Burley Moor.

4 **Turn left** and follow the footpath **south-west** to Horncliffe Well. Cross the stile and **turn right** to follow the wall **north-west** then go through the first gate and continue in the same direction to arrive at a large stone waymarker.

5 **Go north** along the trail to the Twelve Apostles stone circle, then head **north-west** along the trail to the Lanshaw Lad.

6 Follow the stone path downhill; just after crossing Backstone Beck **turn right** to follow the footpath **north-east** along the western side of the beck to the Poetry Seat on the left. Continue downhill and cross the beck by a group of large boulders in the stream bed.

7 **Walk east** until you reach the Dales Way; **turn right** along the trail and walk for **1.1km**, noting the Pancake Stone on the right covered in ancient cup and ring marks.

8 **Turn left** along the waymarked public footpath down to the road and cross to a gate on the other side. Follow the waymarked path across farmland to exit on to a tarmac lane. **Turn right** and walk along the lane; at a sharp right-hand bend take the footpath **straight ahead** into fields. Follow the footpath heading **east** then **south-east** until you reach an iron gate; go through the gate on to a tarmac lane.

9 **Turn right** and walk along the lane; **bear left** just after a recreation field and take the public footpath through trees to emerge on to a road. **Turn left** and walk along the road then **turn right** to return to Burley in Wharfedale Station.

THE TWELVE APOSTLES STONE CIRCLE

THE OLD KEIGHLEY ROAD ACROSS ILKLEY MOOR

19 Ilkley Moor

19km/11.8miles

Seek out the many poems on the Stanza Stones poetry trail, while enjoying the views on this beautiful walk. Do not forget your hat!

Ilkley » Backstone Beck » Thimble Stones » Swastika Stone » Black Hill » Addingham » Ilkley

Start

Ilkley Station. GR: SE 118476.

The Walk

The bustling Yorkshire town of Ilkley is an excellent place to stay and savour the delights of the area. It does not take long to be out on the moors from the cafes and shops of the town centre.

At the beginning of the walk you will find the Beck Stone, the first, or last, of Simon Armitage's poems on the Stanza Stones poetry trail carved into rock in Backstone Beck. The beck makes for a pleasant walk up on to Ilkley Moor. Further up you will find the Poetry Seat and Poetry Postbox to deposit your own thoughts and read those of others about the landscape.

Of course, Ilkely Moor is famous as being the place you must not go without a hat because 'tha's bahn t'catch thi deeath o'cowd' – so says the song. As you reach the top of the moor it is easy to see where the song came from; the wind can take the temperature down even on a sunny day. Just before the Thimble Stones the Puddle Stones – another point on the Stanza Stones poetry trail – can be found. From there the walk drops down into the valley and then heads west past the Swastika Stone, a rock with ancient art engraving. The route then crosses the valley to Addingham, a good place for lunch, before a gentle walk back along the banks of the River Wharfe to Ilkley. The perfect walk for a weekend break.

ILKLEY MOOR

DISTANCE: 19KM/11.8MILES » TOTAL ASCENT: 491M/1,611FT » START GR: SE 118476 » TIME: ALLOW 6 HOURS
SATNAV: LS29 8HF » MAP: OS EXPLORER 297, LOWER WHARFEDALE & WASHBURN VALLEY, 1:25,000
REFRESHMENTS: THE FLEECE, ADDINGHAM; FLYING DUCK, ILKLEY » NAVIGATION: GOOD NAVIGATION SKILLS REQUIRED.

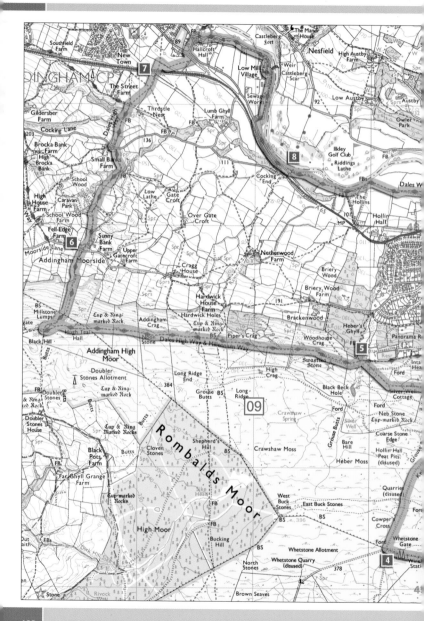

19 ILKLEY MOOR

Directions – Ilkley Moor

⊙ **Turn right** out of Ilkley Station and walk to the junction of Wells Promenade. **Turn left** and walk along the road. Continue on to Wells Road; at the junction with Crossbeck Road take the public footpath **east** along the left-hand side of The Tarn. At the far end by a bench **turn left** to walk through trees to the road. Do not go on to the road but take the footpath up steps, then follow the *Stanza Stone* signposts to reach the Beck Stone by the footbridge.

2 Retrace your steps to the footpath and continue uphill passing the Poetry Seat, part of the Stanza Stones poetry trail, on the way. Continue until you reach a path junction at Gill Head.

3 **Turn left** heading **south** until you reach Lanshaw Lad then **turn right** heading **west** to follow the path past the Ordnance Survey triangulation pillar. Shortly afterwards, just before the Thimble Stones, look out for the Puddle Stones, part of the Stanza Stones poetry trail, then continue in the same direction until a wide track is reached.

4 **Turn right** along the track, passing Cowper's Cross on the left, until you reach the beginning of a road, and a well-made track on the left. **Turn left** along the track passing to the **left** of Silver Well Cottage and exiting on to the moor. Follow the footpath down to some benches at Black Beck.

5 Continue **west** along the footpath, stopping to examine the fenced Swastika Stone overlooking the River Wharfe, and crossing several stiles and gates to arrive at the cairn below Black Hill. **Turn right** and follow the path down Millstone Lumps to the minor road at Addingham Moorside.

6 Go **straight ahead** following the public footpath down a tarmac drive then through a stone squeeze stile leading on to fields. Follow the waymarkers **north-east** passing a caravan park to the left and skirting around Small Banks Farm to a road. Cross the road, going through the gate opposite. Cross fields to a footbridge then **bear right**, across fields to exit on to the A65 on the outskirts of Addingham.

7 Cross the road and walk straight ahead across a field to a hedgerow. **Turn right** along the hedge and halfway along **bear left** to exit the field by a farm gate. Cross the road and **turn left** to walk along the road. **Turn right** at the junction then shortly afterwards **turn right** again. Follow the lane alongside the river to Low Mill Village. Go through the village then **turn left** at a T-junction. Follow the road until you reach a signpost on the left for the *Dales Way*.

8 **Turn left** following the Dales Way along the riverbank and across fields to Ilkley. At the end of the trail by the bridge **turn right** to return to Ilkley Station.

ANCIENT WAYMARK POST ON ILKLEY MOOR

STOODLEY PIKE

20 Hebden Bridge to Marsden

28.7km/17.8miles

Save this wonderful walk for a day when time is not important. Enjoy the open space of the South Pennines.

Hebden Bridge » Stoodley Pike » Blackstone Edge Moor » Dog Hill » Stott Hall Farm » Slaithwaite Moor » Marsden

Start

Hebden Bridge Station. GR: SD 995268.

The Walk

This is a long, linear day walk down the spine of the South Pennines. Park at one end and let the train return you at the end of the walk. The reward for all the effort is some magnificent views, a sense of solitude and the feeling of space. It can be either an introduction to the South Pennines or a revisiting of some of the places enjoyed in the other walks. And with a few special places added, such as the most famous farmhouse in Britain, Stott Hall Farm, sitting right in the middle of the M62. The shock of passing by this place is that it is so quiet even with all the traffic thundering across the Pennines above. When I walked this route, it felt like a culmination of all I had experienced in this superb landscape. It left me with a sense of achievement and satisfaction, and that I had found somewhere new and worthwhile to revisit. I hope you will feel the same.

HEBDEN BRIDGE TO MARSDEN

DISTANCE: 28.7KM/17.8MILES » **TOTAL ASCENT:** 820M/2,690FT » **START GR:** SD 995268 » **TIME:** ALLOW 9 HOURS **SATNAV:** HX7 6JE » **MAP:** OS EXPLORER OL21, SOUTH PENNINES, 1:25,000 » **REFRESHMENTS:** OLD GATE BAR & RESTAURANT, HEBDEN BRIDGE; THE RAILWAY, MARSDEN » **NAVIGATION:** GOOD NAVIGATION SKILLS REQUIRED.

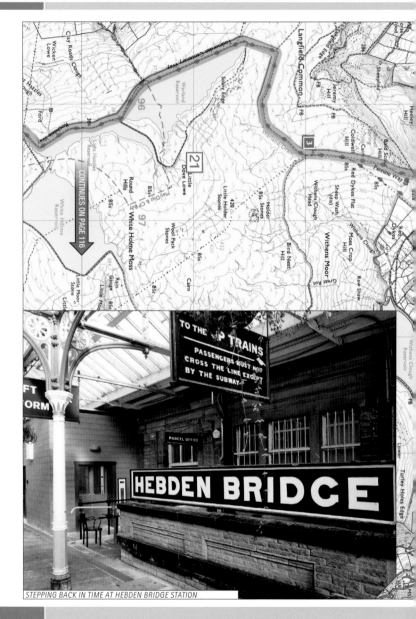

CONTINUES ON PAGE 116

STEPPING BACK IN TIME AT HEBDEN BRIDGE STATION

20 HEBDEN BRIDGE TO MARSDEN

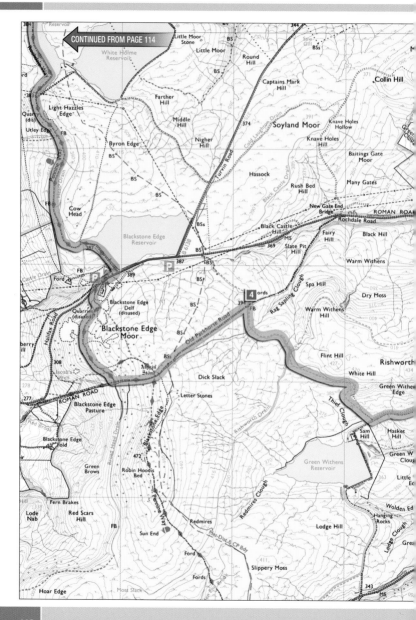

CONTINUED FROM PAGE 114

BANK BOTTOM MILL, MARSDEN

20 HEBDEN BRIDGE TO MARSDEN

CONTINUES ON PAGE 119

Directions – Hebden Bridge to Marsden

> **Turn right** out of Hebden Bridge Station heading **east** on a footpath then **turn right** on to Mayroyd Lane. Continue on under the railway bridge to the end of a row of houses. **Turn right** on to the track that runs behind the houses. Go **straight across** at the first junction then **turn left** at the second junction to Old Chamber. Cross the minor road and go **straight ahead**, heading **south** on a track. **Turn right** up the slope then **turn right** again and follow a wall running uphill. At the top follow the wall **south** past Rake Head to reach Dick's Lane.

2 Walk **south–east** down the walled lane and at the end **turn right** and follow the trail to Stoodley Pike. From the monument follow the edge trail **south–west** until the trail forks by a signpost.

3 **Fork right** heading **south–west** and follow the wide trail to Blackstone Edge Reservoir passing the Rain Stone on the Stanza Stones poetry trail at Light Hazzles Edge. On reaching the A58 **turn right** and walk past the pub then cross the road and join the conduit trail along Blackstone Edge Moor heading generally **south** to a wide track by a fence. **Turn left** heading **east** and follow the old packhorse route to a footbridge above Rag Sapling Clough.

4 **Turn right** to follow the permissive path **south** to Green Withens Reservoir and join the conduit track heading **east.** Where the track turns **south–east** go over the stone bridge and ascend the moor to the Blackwood Edge Road (Path). Follow the path **east** until a wall and ladder stile is reached then **turn right** and follow the footpath **south–east** to exit on to a track by Rishworth Lodge. **Turn left** and follow the track to a minor road.

5 **Turn right** and take the first footpath on the **left** to the A672. Cross the road and descend the road beneath the dam. At the end of the dam take the footpath on the **right** up through a narrow woodland. Cross the access road and ascend the hillside, going through the wrought iron gate, to rejoin the access road and pass by Stott Hall Farm nestling beneath the two carriageways of the M62.

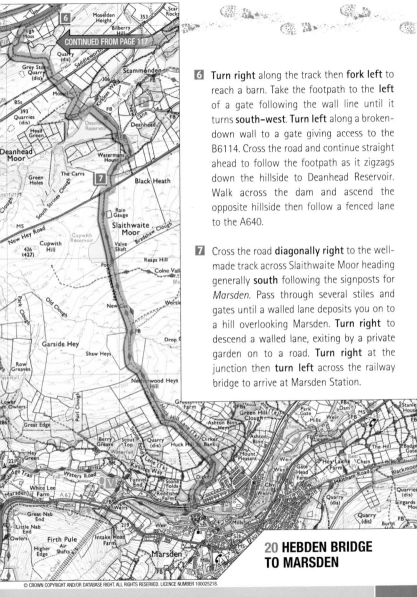

CONTINUED FROM PAGE 117

6 **Turn right** along the track then **fork left** to reach a barn. Take the footpath to the **left** of a gate following the wall line until it turns **south-west**. **Turn left** along a broken-down wall to a gate giving access to the B6114. Cross the road and continue straight ahead to follow the footpath as it zigzags down the hillside to Deanhead Reservoir. Walk across the dam and ascend the opposite hillside then follow a fenced lane to the A640.

7 Cross the road **diagonally right** to the well-made track across Slaithwaite Moor heading generally **south** following the signposts for *Marsden*. Pass through several stiles and gates until a walled lane deposits you on to a hill overlooking Marsden. **Turn right** to descend a walled lane, exiting by a private garden on to a road. **Turn right** at the junction then **turn left** across the railway bridge to arrive at Marsden Station.

20 HEBDEN BRIDGE TO MARSDEN

Appendix

Further Reading

There is so much literature that describes the South Pennines it is difficult to choose specifics. Anything by the Brontë sisters that feature the areas the walks visit will add extra texture to a day. The poetry of Ted Hughes and Simon Armitage reflect the moods and feelings of the moors.

The Gallows Pole
Benjamin Myers
Bluemoose Books, 2017
This recent publication about the Cragg Vale coiners and certainly gives a detailed perspective for walk 11.

Moods of the Brontë Moors
John Morrison
Halsgrove, 2004
This is a wonderful photo essay of the area and its communities.

Fabric of The Hills: The Interwoven Story of Textiles and the Landscape of the South Pennines
Elizabeth Jane Pridmore
Landscape Working Group, 1989
This gives an excellent account of the textile industry in the area.

Early Trackways in The South Pennines
Margaret and David Drake
Pennine Heritage, 1982
This is a fascinating account of the old ways across the moors.

Visitor Information Centres

Halifax	T: 01422 368 725
Haworth	T: 01535 642 329
Hebden Bridge	T: 01422 843 831
Holmfirth	T: 01484 223 200
Ilkley	T: 01943 602 319
Todmorden	T: 01706 818 181

Food & Drink
Cafes

Watersedge Cafe, Marsden	T: 01484 844 298
Hollingworth Lake Visitor Centre Cafe	T: 01706 373 421
Weaving Shed Cafe, Gibson Mill	T: 01422 846 236

Pubs

The Fleece, Holme	T: 01484 683 449
The Clarence, Greenfield	T: 01457 820 200
The Riverhead Brewery Tap, Marsden	T: 01484 844 324
The Top Brink Inn, Lumbutts	T: 01706 812 696

Weather
www.metoffice.gov.uk

Transport and Accommodation
www.southpennines.co.uk
www.yorkshire.com
www.visitlancashire.com
www.visitnorthwest.com

Websites

www.southpennines.co.uk
Contains a wealth of information about the area
including accommodation, transport, history and
the wildlife of the area. It also has an excellent
directory of events, and suggestions.

www.stanzastones.co.uk
The Stanza Stones poetry trail, that so many
of the walks in this guidebook engage with,
is a wonderful way of getting art, people
and landscape to come together.

www.nationaltrust.org.uk/hardcastle-crags
www.nationaltrust.org.uk/marsden-moor-estate
www.peakandnorthern.org.uk

Other Publications

Day Walks in the Peak District:
20 Classic Circular Routes
Norman Taylor & Barry Pope,
Vertebrate Publishing – **www.v-publishing.co.uk**

Day Walks in the Peak District:
20 New Circular Routes
Norman Taylor & Barry Pope,
Vertebrate Publishing – **www.v-publishing.co.uk**

Day Walks in the Yorkshire Dales
Bernard Newman,
Vertebrate Publishing – **www.v-publishing.co.uk**

West Yorkshire Mountain Biking: South Pennine Trails
Benjamin Haworth, Vertebrate Publishing –
www.v-publishing.co.uk

THE GRADE 1 SCRAMBLE OF WILDERNESS GULLY WEST

About the Author

Paul Besley is a writer who started exploring the British landscape while at school in the 1970s. His main focus of work is the interaction between human and land from the Neolithic period to the present day. His work has evolved into the study of how the physical environment imprints itself on humans and how we as a race respond. He lives close to the peat and gritstone of the Peak District with his wife, metalsmith Alison Counsell, their two pet dogs, Monty and Olly, and his Mountain Rescue Search Dog, Scout.

Vertebrate Publishing

At Vertebrate Publishing we publish books to inspire adventure.

It's our rule that the only books we publish are those that we'd want to read or use ourselves. We endeavour to bring you beautiful books that stand the test of time and that you'll be proud to have on your bookshelf for years to come.

The Peak District was the inspiration behind our first books. Our offices are situated on its doorstep, minutes away from world-class climbing, biking and hillwalking. We're driven by our own passion for the outdoors, for exploration, and for the natural world; it's this passion that we want to share with our readers.

We aim to inspire everyone to get out there. We want to connect readers – young and old – with the outdoors and the positive impact it can have on well-being. We think it's particularly important that young people get outside and explore the natural world, something we support through our publishing programme.

As well as publishing award-winning new books, we're working to make available many out-of-print classics in both print and digital formats. These are stories that we believe are unique and significant; we want to make sure that they continue to be shared and enjoyed.
www.v-publishing.co.uk

AN ANCIENT HOLLOW WAY UP ON TO THE MOORS